Spiritual Fitness

Spiritual Fitness

*Christian character in a
consumer society*

Graham Tomlin

continuum
LONDON • NEW YORK

Continuum

The Tower Building
11 York Road
London SE1 7NX

80 Maiden Lane, Suite 704
New York
NY 10038

www.continuumbooks.com

First published 2006

British Library Cataloguing-in-Publication Data
A catalogue record for this book is available from the British Library.

ISBN 0–8264–8677–0

Typeset by Kenneth Burnley, Wirral, Cheshire
Printed and bound by MPG Books, Bodmin, Cornwall

Contents

In grateful memory of

Emrys and Ruth Wynn Owen

Introduction

Several years ago I wrote a book called *The Provocative Church*. Its basic idea was that the best evangelism happens as the answer to a question. Trying to talk about the Christian faith to someone who is not remotely interested is like trying to get blood out of a stone. It's a whole lot easier talking to someone who has seen or experienced something that has intrigued him and made him wonder whether this Christian thing has something in it after all. The question is, therefore, how do we provoke the question? How do Christians get people who normally dismiss faith to begin to ask whether there might be a God who takes a real interest in them after all? The answer is the kingdom of God. When people experience the reality of the kingdom, life as it was always meant to be, under the strong and gentle rule of God, that is when they begin to experience a longing for something else, something we once knew as a human race. And so the church's first task is not actually evangelism, or just getting the words right, but displaying the life of the kingdom in its own life and community, which in turn will provoke the questions that lead to effective evangelism.

As I travelled around speaking about these ideas, I found again and again the same question being asked, and I found myself asking it too. What kind of life would really provoke the question? What style of life would be so distinctive, so attractive, that it would make a whole society or culture begin to take notice and want to have it for themselves? Although the book did sketch some answers, it only began to do so. There was more work to be done.

At the same time, something else was going on, not so much in my spiritual or intellectual horizons, but in my physical make-up.

I have a bad back: not chronic, but every now and again it gives me real grief for a week or so and makes me hobble around like a 90-year-old. Thinking I should do more than just grimace and bear it, I was looking to see if there was some kind of treatment I could undertake. One day a leaflet dropped through our door offering a class in Pilates, a form of focused physical exercise, at a physiotherapy centre just around the corner from our home. Dimly remembering that a friend had recommended Pilates for bad backs, I duly sent off my cheque and signed up for the five-week class.

When I turned up at the centre one Wednesday evening, I found myself in an upstairs room with six other people dressed in jogging trousers, most of whom also seemed to have dodgy backs, waiting for the instructor to arrive. When she did, I imme-diately noticed something. As she moved across the room, she did so with a remarkable poise and balance. She seemed to float rather than walk, and appeared to have an elegance and grace which our hobbling bodies lacked.

She proceeded to explain how Pilates works, or at least the form of it she was teaching. By strengthening the key inner muscles around the stomach and lower back, using a combin-ation of breathing, stretching and relaxation, a kind of core stability can be developed which then frees the rest of the body to act normally. If these muscles are undeveloped, the spine starts taking strain it was never meant to, leading to the kind of dis-comfort most of us were experiencing.

More vividly, she began to show us some exercises. One involved trying to stand on one leg for a period of time. The scene was quite comical, with all of us wobbling precariously before toppling over onto two legs again after about ten seconds. Our teacher, however, was able to accomplish this without any problem whatsoever. She stood there on one leg for as long as she wanted, as if silently wondering what our problem was. She showed us various exercises, all of which seemed to come nat-urally to her, with hardly any effort at all. For us these were a huge physical strain, and we still couldn't do them for long.

It wasn't that she was putting more effort into it than we were – in fact it was the opposite. She seemed to be putting less effort into it, but her body had become trained, schooled in such exercises, so that she was able to perform them without any trouble. The key to it gradually became clear. It wasn't just a case of trying harder. It was all to do with these core muscles. By a series of simple exercises, repeated during the week between the classes, we began to find our own 'core' or 'centre' strengthening as well. As the weeks went by, we found we could do some of the things she had seemed to achieve so effortlessly that first Wednesday. Even I could stand on one leg for quite a while without toppling over. Even I was beginning to gain this balance, uprightness and poise which had seemed so foreign at first. And my back was beginning to get better.

Classes in life

Wednesday evenings that winter were proving busy. After my Pilates class, I had to rush off to church where I had agreed to help on an Alpha course, an introductory programme for people who had shown an interest in Christianity. I was giving some of the talks, leading a group, and helping the people on the course discuss and discover Christian faith for themselves. As the weeks went by there, I couldn't help comparing the two experiences.

Both were set courses over a limited period of time, with a clear end in sight. Both offered transformation of some kind if you saw the course through to the end and took it seriously. Both enabled individuals to explore a new way of moving (in one case) and living (in another). On both, I found people gradually warming to what they were doing, and finding real change happening in their lives as a result.

At the same time, a plush new health and fitness centre opened up quite near where we lived and many of our friends had joined up, taking part with varying degrees of enthusiasm and commitment. I began to wonder what the church might have to learn from such things as the Pilates class and the gym. This book is the result.

It struck me that large numbers of people put huge amounts of energy and time into developing their physical health and fitness, whether motivated by pain, vanity or the desire for long life. What would happen if Christians started doing the same with their spiritual health and fitness? I could see and admire friends who had taken their physical health seriously and were slowly developing new habits and a new shape to their bodies – you could tell the difference over time, both from their former flabby selves and from others who didn't give too much attention to matters of physical well-being. Could I really see many Christians in whom such change was visible?

I also began to wonder what would happen if churches started to offer classes to help people develop spiritual health and fitness, just as gyms did in the physical realm. They would, of course, be different in a number of important ways. At the same time, however, a course similar to Alpha but focused more on developing spiritual health and strength in a distinctively Christian way might have genuine appeal to people who were interested in developing not just physically but also spiritually.

It then occurred to me that this is just what the church has done over the centuries and, furthermore, you could even see the whole of Christian theology as focused on enabling people to grow into their full potential as human beings, created and redeemed by God. And of course the next stage was to begin to think what the church would look like if it began to be organized around the aim of enabling people to grow into full spiritual and human health.

At the same time, endless political and social debates were going on about how to discourage antisocial behaviour and improve social cohesiveness. Is multiculturalism the right way to go about it, letting different cultures coexist independently of one another, or should we try to blend these into a more unified culture, eroding the distinctives of each cultural group in a plural society? In the light of social, ethnic and religious tension, how can government order a properly functioning, peaceful society where social relations are characterized by respect and harmony, not conflict and violence? The more these debates continued, the less it seemed that governments alone could solve them. 'Faith-based' solutions were mulled over, but often they were single-focus community projects. Was there something that faith itself could do to answer these questions? If the church became a place as dedicated to developing spiritual health and strength as gyms are to developing physical well-being, might they hold the clue to building a cohesive and coherent society?

Thanks are due to a number of people who have helped me develop these ideas, who read early drafts of the manuscript and corrected me where I was wrong, or added new insights. I owe a special debt to Tim and Kate Goodacre, Richard and Dianne Bayfield, Paul Zaphiriou, John Searle, Hector and Caroline Sants and the post-Alpha group that met in their home, on whom some of these ideas were tried out. I am grateful too for the staff and students at Wycliffe Hall, colleagues and friends at Holy Trinity Brompton, and of course Janet, Sam and Siân, my favourite people in the world. The book is dedicated to the memory of two people who exemplified real Christian spiritual goodness and health, and who will always remain in our hearts.

Chapter 1

Church in a culture of choice

Everyone today agrees that the church is failing. Even though it may be growing phenomenally in other parts of the world, in Europe at least its days seem to be numbered.

It is not hard to find the reason. It is not primarily because people no longer believe in God, are no longer interested in spiritual things, or have grave intellectual objections to Christianity, or even because they are protesting against the abuse of power in the church. It is largely because they have better things to do with their time. Church for many people simply feels boring, irrelevant and unnecessary. And today's culture offers a whole raft of more effective and attractive ways to fill Sunday mornings or find spiritual enlightenment. Why would I want to get involved in church when I can read the Sunday papers and find inner peace through yoga?

Church just doesn't seem to display a very attractive product. It doesn't offer people what they want. Nick Spencer, a researcher and writer at the London Institute for Contemporary Christianity, interviewing people about attitudes to church, found that church was an unattractive consumer choice. As one person put it: 'The church should reflect what we want. The church should not dictate to us that you can get married, or you can't get married. We want to get married. We are consumers of the church.'[1] Are they right? Should the church be worried about the fact that it no longer seems to offer anything of relevance or attraction to many contemporary people in the West? Or should it simply carry on doing what it has always done, regardless of whether people like it or not, waiting for a change in the cultural weather that brings the numbers flocking back through the doors again?

It is a central contention of this book that the church should be concerned about the fact that people no longer find it necessary, compelling or relevant. It is often said that Christians are called not to be relevant but to be faithful. That is true, but it is also true that if they are faithful they will also be relevant. Of course the church is called to 'do what it has always done'. Yet the problem is that in the church we have often forgotten what we have always done, what we are good at, and what we are here for. We have largely forgotten that we are here not just to grow big, to influence politics, or to be an agent for social change. We are here to enable people and communities to be restored into the image of God. And if we begin to learn what that means, there can be no agenda more relevant, attractive and compelling in the world.

Yet that is perhaps to get ahead of ourselves. Is it really the church's job to be relevant? If church is a failing business in contemporary life, should it be worried about the competition? Is a desire for relevance selling out the gospel for short-term popularity? Should the church pay any attention at all to the spirit of the age? How should the church respond to a consumer culture?

Church in a consumer society

The mailshot is one of the prices we pay for living in an age of easy communication. A mysteriously personalized letter drops through your letterbox, urging you to sign up for a new credit card, book a weekend bargain holiday, purchase an eyebrow-trimmer or retractable garden hose. Normally they end up in the bin, but occasionally one catches your eye and elicits a sale. In the futuristic film *Minority Report*, Tom Cruise is trying to escape a plot to kill him. Racing through a large shopping mall, he is surrounded by hologram-style figures advertising various products. Even more scarily, he hears voices, addressing him directly by name, inviting him to purchase different kinds of scent, clothing or food. What would it be like to live in a world where we could be targeted inside our heads?

Some would say we are already halfway there. To turn on the TV, to browse the Internet, or to open a magazine is to be bombarded with alluring images all aiming at one thing – to encourage us to buy into their product and consume. At times it seems as if our main function in society is to do exactly that. We define ourselves not as workers, producers of goods, or contributors to society, but as consumers of what other people produce.

Consumerism is one of the central features of life in 'advanced' Western societies. Some would say it was the most central and defining feature of the 'postmodern' world. As David Lyon puts it, 'If postmodernity means anything, it means the consumer society.'[2]

At some point after the end of World War II, a new kind of society began to emerge in the West. Fredric Jameson describes it as involving the following:

> New types of consumption; planned obsolescence, an ever more rapid rhythm of fashion and styling changes; the penetration of advertising, television and the media to a hitherto unparalleled degree within society; the replacement of the old tension between city and country, centre and province, the growth of the great networks of superhighways and the arrival of automobile culture.[3]

As the Iron Curtain fell in Europe in 1989, consumer capitalism spread its wings eastwards, and critics such as the American political economist Francis Fukuyama were announcing the 'end of history' as we know it. His point was not, of course, that no historical events could happen from then on, but that 'history' in the Enlightenment sense of the word as envisaged by Hegel and Marx – history as progressing towards a better society – had now come to an end. Western society had now reached its final destination in the sense that it no longer had any fundamental internal contradictions, and all the big questions had been finally settled. In Fukuyama's argument, all opposition to liberal democracy with its attendant capitalist, consumerist economies seemed to have disappeared.[4]

Fukuyama's optimism (if that's what it is) has been strongly disputed, yet it points nonetheless to a defining feature of the culture in which the Western church lives today: it inhabits a society of consumers. The church may not like it, but that's the way it is. How the church responds to such a culture is vital. In any culture or age, if the church does not try to understand its culture and the spirit that inhabits it, it tends to blend into it. To fail to recognize the idols to which it will be tempted to bow down is to risk a subtle and hardly noticed worship of those very gods. A church in any given cultural setting needs both a strong sense of its own identity and a shrewd awareness of the trends and temptations that surround it if it is to be faithful to its true Lord, Jesus Christ.

So, should the church give people what they want, or make people want what it gives?

Consumerism and Christianity

There is, of course, a negative side to consumerism. Consumerism feeds off dissatisfaction and so cultivates it mercilessly. It creates a constant thirst for more and a need for new experiences. Despite the protestations of advertising, the last thing an aggressive retailer wants is a fully satisfied customer. Satisfied customers are content with what they have and so they don't buy. If people don't buy, then the economic structure of consumerism begins to falter. As the British sociologist Zygmunt Bauman points out, capitalist societies encourage consumers to be fickle, restless and never entirely satisfied: 'Ideally nothing should be embraced by a consumer firmly, nothing should command a commitment until death us do part, no needs should be seen as fully satisfied, no desires considered ultimate.'[5]

Consumerism also has a more sinister tendency to destroy community. If I define myself as a consumer first and foremost, then I am entirely free to choose how I look, how I dress, and how I spend my spare time. Consumerism is fundamentally about making choices. And, of course, the more I make my own ever more personalized decisions about my leisure pursuits, wardrobe or morality, the more they will tend to make me different from my neighbours. It will isolate me in the little world of my own closely guarded 'freedom to choose'.

A third problem with consumerism is that, taken to extremes, it makes you worry. When you go to a supermarket, you are faced with not just one type of breakfast cereal, but a whole aisle full of them. You don't just choose one type of dishwashing liquid or chocolate bar, but you have to take your pick between 30 different kinds. Those choices are relatively easy – you get one that you know and tend to stick with it. When it comes to picking a mobile phone, it begins to get ridiculous. Not only do you have to choose the phone itself, deciding between different shapes, colours, capacities and so on (in a recent catalogue I looked at, there were around 120 to choose from). You also have to choose the tariff you want to use it on. Do you pay a monthly sum? Just for the units you use? Do you go for one with free text messages or email? One that you can use abroad? One that gives you unlimited calls at weekends, or just the regular deal? With large purchases like choosing a car or even a house, the stakes become higher and the choices more numerous still.

If you really were to investigate every single purchasing decision thoroughly, you would probably do nothing else. When there is too much choice, it can become paralysing. Barry Schwartz, in *The Paradox of Choice*, points out how stressful consumer society is when it imposes so many choices upon us. Multiplying options to choose from actually decreases rather than increases levels of satisfaction among consumers, as it introduces levels of anxiety over whether we are making the best choice, or, having made it, whether we could have got a better deal elsewhere.[6] Consumerism gone wild actually leads to unhappiness and frustration. As Schwartz puts it, 'there comes a point at which opportunities become so numerous that we feel overwhelmed. Instead of feeling in control, we feel unable to cope.'[7]

Furthermore, there might be a more specifically Christian

objection to consumerism. What people want may not be what they need. People may want a new car, fame or an exotic holiday, but what they really need is the forgiveness of sins. Of course churches won't be offering free Mercedes or trips to Barbados, but they do sometimes promise happiness, success and affluence. But is that to pander to fallen and therefore twisted desire? Is that to offer false promises and fake religion? Is it to address felt needs and not real ones?

Good consumption?

So is consumerism all bad? Or is there another side to it? Freedom to choose is a positive and perhaps even essential feature of well-being. Most of us would find a society that gave you no choice at all pretty oppressive and lacking in colour. Having to wear standard-issue government-approved products, such as the blue Mao suits that became *de rigueur* in communist China during the Cultural Revolution, would not be like a popular fashion move. Moreover, the New Testament, not to mention the Old, presents us with a God who is the source of variety and diversity. He is one who 'richly provides us with everything for our enjoyment' (1 Tim. 6.17). He also gives us choices to be made. He urges his people to choose whom they will serve (Josh. 24.15), and again and again urges them to learn how to discern good from evil, and to choose the former. We are made with bodies that are not self-sufficient, but sustain themselves by the consumption of food, drink and air to breathe, and keep warm and modest through clothing. We were made, in part at least, to consume.

In addition to this, religion itself, perhaps especially Christianity in the Western world, has wittingly or unwittingly gone along with a consumer mentality. Many Christians moving to a new town will shop around until they find a church that suits them. It is less likely now than it used to be that they will look for one particular denomination. Instead they will tend to look for such things as inspiring worship, stimulating preaching, good youth and children's ministry and ease of parking. Religious life in the contemporary world is effectively consumerist.[8] Religion has become commoditized and people take their pick between the options on offer. It is not uncommon to find people selecting the parts of different religions they like and putting them together into some strange amorphous whole, mixing a little bit of Hinduism with some Buddhist meditation, Christian prayer and New Age crystals.

It is certainly true that consumerism is not a matter of mere materialism. Although some Christians have argued vociferously against consumerism as if it is just acquisitiveness disguised, there is clearly a lot more going on than that. Consumption is not just shopping for things, it is also shopping for meaning. Cars are bought not just for their functionality as a means of getting around, but for their value as status symbols. When I buy a suit, I am not just buying a piece of clothing to keep me warm or clean. I am buying a product that says something about me that I want to make sure I say. When I wear it to an interview, a social reception or a funeral, it says that I am respectable, trustworthy, well groomed and orderly. All this may or may not be true of me, but the suit says it anyway. And depending on which kind of suit I buy, it will say different things. A sober, dark-coloured two-piece affair with creased trousers and two jacket buttons will give an impression of conservativism and reliability. A white suit with no jacket lapels, buttons up to the neck and 'Georgio Armani' on the label will convey something different altogether.

Shopping is increasingly a way not just of feeding and clothing ourselves, but of defining who we are. When a teenager shops, she chooses a particular 'look' by choosing Fatface over Gap. By changing the fascia or ringtone on her mobile phone she also chooses to emphasize a particular identity by the style or message it conveys. We construct new images and identities all the time by what we buy. As the sociologist David Lyon puts it, 'Postmodern consumers constantly "try on" not only new clothes, new perfumes, but new identities, fresh personalities, different partners.'[9]

Besides shopping for meaning, consumers increasingly shop for experiences. Advertisers cannily present their products not as 'things' – after all, there is a contemporary yearning for an uncluttered life that aspires to effortless simplicity rather than grubby 1980s materialism. Cars are sold not primarily by presenting detailed descriptions of their engine capacity, the number of cylinders or the diameter of the wheels, but by presenting an experience. It might be driving through an expansive empty countryside, a family day out, or a sexual seduction. The implicit message is that buying this car will give you this kind of experience. Hotels or holidays are advertised not functionally with information about price, or the number of beds or swimming pools, but as offering a vision of escape, relaxation or adventure, or simply giving you more to talk about at parties. The ads simply present the experience and try to draw you into it.

Consumerism is not simple. Nor is it simply bad. It is merely the way in which we say who we are. In one sense, Christians who buy 'What Would Jesus Do' bracelets, put fish stickers on their cars, or buy crucifixes to wear round their necks are doing exactly the same thing as shoppers who wear Dolce and Gabbana clothes – they are choosing to say something about who they are and where their identity lies. It is much the same as the centuries-old Christian practice of receiving the mark of the cross in ash on the forehead on Ash Wednesday, or the mark of the cross in baptism. These are signs or brand markings that tell us who we are.

So consumerism is perhaps in itself neutral. As Zygmunt Bauman says, 'Consumer society is a different instrumentality, but in itself, it is neither moral nor immoral, like any other.' If he is right, then consumerism simply describes the nature of the culture in which the church is called to exist and bear witness. Any given culture will always be a mixture of good and bad, God-derived goodness and evil-inspired deception. Consumer culture is no different. To be sure, if we only define people in terms of their existence as consumers, then we have missed something crucial about human beings – that they are called into relationship with God and with each other. We are defined more by the things we choose than by the act of choosing itself. We may not be *merely* consumers, but we are consumers nonetheless.

Consuming religion

The bottom line is that if the church exists in a consumer society, it has to be able to deliver. If people will choose – at its most basic, choose what they want to do on Sunday mornings or evenings – then the church, whether it likes it or not, is instantly in a situation of competition. It competes with supermarket shopping, football, car-washing, car boot sales and a myriad of other weekend activities which might be more attractive than turning up at church.

Now we are not used to this. For centuries the church had a near monopoly on the spiritual sphere, on the big questions of life. Yet in saying we are now in an age where, to put it bluntly, the church is engaged in competition for attention, is only to say that we are back where we started. The church was born into an age where it was in competition with pagan religion, which had its own answers to the questions of human existence. First-century Greco-Roman paganism was every bit as pluralistic as modern societies. It had its panoply of gods you could choose between, and it didn't really matter which one you worshipped as long as you bought into the overall system. Each town had its selection of temples, just like our towns have different supermarkets or chain stores. The church simply had to show that it could do better than the pagans. It had to demonstrate that it could offer something more compelling, convincing and ultimately satisfying than anything pagan religion could offer.

Some years ago our son, who was heavily into football, started playing in the local boys' leagues. These games, of course, always happened on Sunday mornings. We faced the classic Christian parents' dilemma: should we insist he goes to church on Sunday morning? If we did, we risked banning him from the most important time of his week, cutting him off from his friends, and us from the other parents we had come to know on the touchline. Or should we let him play, and find some other way of giving him (and us) spiritual input and fellowship? Was culture going to toe the line for church, or was church going to adapt to the culture? We decided on the latter. After a fair bit of discussion, we persuaded our local church to let us begin a Sunday evening group for young kids who played sport on Sunday mornings. Rightly or wrongly, here was the church adapting to its place in a consumer society.

The problem is that, going on current figures, certainly in Western Europe, church is not an attractive consumer choice. The facts are well known, so there is no need to labour them, but to take just one statistic, total church attendance in Britain fell from a figure of around 5.4 million in 1979 to 3.8 million in 1998. Most of that fall has been within the 'institutional' churches, for example the Church of England, Roman Catholics, Methodists and so on.[10] Many people are voting with their feet – leaving the buildings and not coming back.

Why is church boring?

For some the problem is a lack of evangelism. If we simply did more of it, then the problem would go away and people would start returning to the church in droves. The difficulty here is that the figures don't bear this out. On the advice of many Third World leaders, the Church of England declared the 1990s to be a 'Decade of Evangelism'. The results were not encouraging. Here are just some of the changes that took place in that church through the 1990s:

Adult attendance	Down 14%
Child attendance	Down 28%
Confirmations	Down 43%
Electoral rolls	Down 13%
Stipendiary clergy	Down 15%
Marriages in church	Down 46%[11]

The only thing that went up was the average age of committed Anglicans. Some would say that despite the hype, there wasn't any more evangelism during the 1990s than at any other time.

Big-name crusades of the Billy Graham or Luis Palau variety, which were the dominant mode of mass evangelism from the 1950s to the 1980s, seem to have had their day. Alpha and other 'process' courses in evangelism (Alpha is by far the biggest) have seen significant success in bringing many to faith in Christ since the 1990s. It hardly bears thinking what the last 15 years would have been like for the church without Alpha, and yet even this has not entirely stemmed the haemorrhaging of people from church. It has slowed decline, but has not yet reversed it. As fast as new Christians come in through the front door, others are leaving through the back. Alpha still remains one of the key tools in evangelism in the contemporary scene, yet there is more work to be done on what happens after people have come to faith on Alpha, and how people are sustained in long-term Christian life. To say we need more evangelism may be true, but it still remains to be seen what kind of evangelism is needed and what happens after people are converted.

Others would say the problem is liturgical. The church is wedded to outmoded forms of worship that need radical change if the modern/postmodern world is to be won back to Christ. Again the difficulty is that much of this has been tried. The Roman Catholic Church moved towards vernacular liturgies in the 1960s, and the Church of England has had two new service books in the past 25 years. Decline continues in both. More recently, new expressions of church have emerged, trying out various kinds of innovative liturgy and forms of worship. Yet at present, in the UK at least, they mostly remain small and fragile, and while this development holds much promise its exact shape is still unclear.[12] Many larger churches have done away with older forms of liturgy and embrace a wide variety of styles, yet even these would tend to say, when asked, that the form of service used is not the central issue. It helps to have something which people relate to when they come through the door, but there needs to be something more which draws them to enter in the first place.

So, if we live in a consumer society, and consumerism isn't all bad, should we simply try to give people what they want? This strategy tends to take two different forms in church life. One is to dress up the Christian gospel in contemporary clothes, so all that is considered 'external' to the core of the faith is up for negotiation and change. Styles of music in church mimic those which the 'target audience' like to listen to on their radio stations every day at home or in the car. Film, video projection and visual stimuli are used far more often to cater for a generation used to receiving information through TV and computer screens rather than books. New churches are built like lecture theatres or cinemas rather than the great Gothic structures of the past. Church leaders look more like business executives than pastors, with ties rather than dog collars and all the trappings of a CEO in a major corporation. All that feels culturally alien in the church's liturgy or preaching style or presentation is adapted to fit the desires and instincts of a new generation. The message remains pretty much the same, but the packaging looks very different.

The other approach is to tailor the traditional message and attendant Christian behaviour to what the consumer wants. In this strategy, the awkward bits of traditional Christian theology or morality are sidelined, to make it more believable or manageable. If the incarnation is considered as no longer believable by any rational person, then it is quietly jettisoned and replaced by something more amenable. If the resurrection or the virgin birth seem a bit too much to take and stretch the credulity of scientifically conditioned people, then it is OK just to treat them as optional myths for a less enlightened age, with purely symbolic rather than literal meaning. A further move tackles the difficult demands of traditional Christian discipleship, and treats them as optional as well. Whether it concerns fasting, spiritual disciplines, regular giving of money to the poor, sexual self-control or avoiding harmful habits, if the customer is king and the customer doesn't want to toe the line, then the line must be stretched.

Different Christian readers will feel uncomfortable with different parts of the list of topics above. Some will feel angry about the surrender of some crucial parts of traditional Christian worship and liturgy. Others will feel offended by an abandonment of classic Christian theology. Some will feel that ethical flexibility has gone too far in embracing practices until now thought to be outside the bounds of authentic Christian behaviour. Still others will feel that the church has failed to adapt sufficiently to contemporary ethical culture and is fighting a losing battle by sticking to outdated rules. This isn't the place to debate all those issues. However, it is the place to ask the question of how the church can meet the challenge of a consumer culture without losing its soul.

Meeting true needs

Is it possible for the church to be true to itself *and* offer something of value to the consumers of contemporary western societies? Or, by acknowledging the reality of consumerism and trying to meet the needs and desires of those consumers, will it inevitably compromise itself? The church often seems caught between two alternatives: capitulating to the spirit of the age, entailing an abandonment of all that makes Christianity distinctive and interesting, or retiring into its own little religious world, cut off from and increasingly ignored by a culture that seeks and finds what it wants elsewhere. Is there another way?

The basic contention of this chapter is that while there are dangers in a consumerist mindset, ultimately there need not be a contradiction between meeting needs and the truth of the gospel. At its heart, the gospel is addressed to people as God has made them.

The clue to all this is in the Christian doctrine of creation. C. S. Lewis once pointed out that it is no accident that on the one hand we are creatures who desire food, drink, sex, friendship and the like, and on the other hand such things do actually exist. Our desires are sometimes a clue to how we are made. They are not an infallible guide, as human desire (at least as Christians understand it) is fallen and disordered, but they are a guide nonetheless. The trick is to distinguish between disordered, sinful desires and created, God-given ones. We should expect to find both in human experience, and a key task of Christian theology is to be able to tell the difference between them. St Augustine taught that 'we look for happiness, not in you, but in what you have created'. What is sinful is not desire in itself, but thinking we can satisfy our deepest human desires somewhere else than in God. So one of the most crucial tasks for the church today, and a task this book tries to undertake, is to identify what form the basic human desire for God takes, particularly in contemporary culture, and to think about how the church can address those desires, enabling people to find the living God who alone can satisfy, heal and deliver. We have already seen how, underneath the desire for a new pair of jeans, whiter teeth or a new set of golf clubs, there is something deeper going on, a search for meaning and identity. Christians will go further and say that deeper still there is a desire for God, which although weakened and damaged by human sin, still has a habit of breaking out in different forms and shapes, if only we can see what those are.

If it is true that we are created by a good and generous God, and that we were made to live in relationship with him, then deep within the human heart we must not be surprised if we find just that – a desire for God. It won't always, or even often, be expressed in those terms, but the Christian doctrine of creation tells us we must recognize it for what it is, however much it may seem like a desire to find significance in something else. We can go still further. If we were made to bear God's image, which means that we are meant to act like him, behave like him and even feel like him, then this desire for God will take the form of a desire to be like him. We might well find that people in their best moments do desire to share the characteristics of God who is love, who displays faithfulness, who is patient, kind and persevering. They might well want to learn how to love, to hope, to trust and to be wise. They will want these things because deep down they know these are precisely the things we need to live well. What do you need to hold a difficult marriage together, to keep caring for disobedient and ungrateful children, to achieve something worthwhile and lasting in life? You need to learn love, patience, forgiveness, perseverance and faithfulness.

If that is the case, and if local churches are capable of enabling people to acquire the qualities that reflect the nature of God and to live well, then they will not only provide something which self-confessed consumers know they need to survive the rest of their lives. Those churches will also be true to their very nature – communities dedicated to the worship of God, Father, Son and Holy Spirit, worship which consists primarily of lives that reflect his very nature and glory.

If churches became known as places where you could learn how to love, to trust, to hope, to forgive, to gain wisdom for life, then they might begin to be attractive, perhaps even necessary, places to belong to. Paradoxically, it is not making Christianity easier to follow that will help it thrive again, but making it harder. Only a distinct form of discipleship that offers real transformation will seem worth it. Shirley Williams, the veteran British politician, when asked why she converted to Christianity as a Roman Catholic, replied, 'I'm a Catholic because it made the greatest demands.'[13]

First, however, we need to take a closer look at the way spiritual desires are expressed today. What form does the deep human desire for God take in contemporary society, and what might that tell us about the shape the church needs to take?

Notes

1   Nick Spencer, *Beyond Belief: Barriers and Bridges to Faith Today* (London: LICC, 2003).
2   David Lyon, *Postmodernity* (Buckingham: Open University, 1994), p. 68.

3 Fredric Jameson, 'Postmodernism and Consumer Society', in *Postmodernism and Its Discontents: Theories, Practices*, E. Ann Kaplan, ed. (London: Verso, 1988), p. 28.

4 Francis Fukuyama, *The End of History and the Last Man* (London: Penguin, 1992).

5 Zygmunt Bauman, *Globalization: The Human Consequences, Themes for the 21st Century* (Cambridge: Polity, 1998), p. 81.

6 Barry Schwartz, *The Paradox of Choice: Why More Is Less* (New York: HarperCollins, 2004).

7 *Ibid.*, p. 104.

8 Peter Berger first suggested this theme in *The Social Reality of Religion* (Harmondsworth: Penguin, 1969). It is explored in more detail in David Lyon, *Jesus in Disneyland* (Cambridge: Polity, 2000).

9 Lyon, *Jesus in Disneyland*, p. 79.

10 Peter Brierley, *The Tide Is Running Out: What the English Church Attendance Survey Reveals* (London: Christian Research, 2000), pp. 32–4.

11 Bob Jackson, *Hope for the Church: Contemporary Strategies for Growth, Explorations* (London: Church House Publishing, 2002).

12 See the Church of England report, The Archbishops Council, *Mission-Shaped Church: Church Planting and Fresh Expressions of Church in a Changing Context, Mission and Public Affairs* (London: 2004).

13 Interview in *Third Way*, April 2004, p. 19.

Chapter 2

Body and soul

If people don't go to church, where do they go? Get out of bed early on a Sunday morning in many a city, look outside the window, and you are likely to see people heading out of their houses, dressed ready for their usual Sunday morning activity, as they have always done. But increasingly those people will be heading not for their neighbourhood church, but for their local gym.

Physical fitness has come a long way. In Victorian and Edwardian times, physical fitness came through 'games', played largely at school, which built noble character and physical strength. This was also a way of developing the sterling qualities needed by the upper classes in public schools to aid them in running the empire.[1] It moved on into regimented school exercise programmes where whole classes would learn well-rehearsed drills involving marching and various gymnastic movements, performing them regularly as a means of physical exercise. Such drills were seen as vital in preparing the nation's youth for military service.[2]

When I was at school in the 1970s, Physical Education consisted of 40 minutes in the school gym. This was a cold, bare, grim room, with wooden climbing bars around the walls, ropes hanging from the ceiling, vaulting horses and medicine balls in the corners. We wore baggy vests and ill-fitting shorts, with not a leotard in sight. PE was a welcome break from maths or biology, but few of us really looked forward to it. No one would ever dream of doing it voluntarily in their spare time.

Now, gyms are as different from this as you can imagine. They are clean, bright and warm. Sophisticated machines lie in ranks to develop every conceivable part of your body. TV screens line the walls to prevent boredom, suitable rhythmic music sounds from the speakers. They look far more like comfortable restaurants than the torture chamber that passed as a gym in my school. In the UK alone, the health and fitness industry is now worth around £700 million and is predicted to reach a value of £1.6 billion by 2008. More than 5 million new people joined fitness centres in the UK in 2003 (compare that to the mere 1.2 million who go to church on Christmas Day in Britain). That figure of 5 million is a 12 per cent increase on the figure for 2000, and numbers are predicted to grow year on year for the foreseeable future.

If increasing numbers of people are voting with their feet and heading for the gym rather than church, can we learn anything from this? If this is one of the forms taken by the contemporary search for fulfilment and well-being, might there be something we have to listen to here?

The perfect body

People go to gyms for two basic reasons – either because they have a creaking body, or because they want to lose weight. Gyms promise physical health and long life. They also claim a large place in our aspiration for beauty and attraction, offering the prospect of sculpting a body to change our lives.

To live in any developed Western society today is to be constantly bombarded with images of what our bodies are supposed to look like. Go into any newsagent and you don't have to look at the top shelf to be presented with a huge range of magazine covers on which strut tanned, slimline men and women. With not an ounce of fat in sight, the women are young, have flat stomachs and smooth, bronzed skin. The men, also young of course, have tight muscles, the classic V-shaped torso and the ubiquitous six-pack. The faces may look different, but the bodies are much the same. And the message is clear: this is what we are all supposed to look like. Celebrity magazines display an array of similarly formed people, and indulge a bizarre interest in the changing shape of their bodies. A photo showing a celebrity with cellulite, putting on weight, or becoming alarmingly skinny becomes news. Details of their workout programmes, how long they spend exercising and the diets they are on somehow fascinate us. Turn on the TV, and it's much the same. Our culture has a very clear idea of what a perfect body looks like. It reinforces that image again and again, with role models displayed everywhere you look in the all-pervading media.

So pervasive is this image of the perfect body that it seems churlish to question it. As it happens, there is much to suggest that the story is more culturally specific than we think. Not every civilization sees it this way. There is, of course, no absolute objective rule laid down that says slim bodies are beautiful and fat ones are ugly. In many developing countries where poverty and hunger are rife, large girth is a status symbol – a sign that you have succeeded in life and a token of beauty. In the affluent West, where few go hungry, the slim body is the status symbol, the mark of success and a richly attractive life. Historically, our idea of the beautiful body is relative too: a glance at the paintings of Rubens or Velásquez, for example, shows how a fuller, rounded, pale white body was all the rage in the seventeenth century. Tanned skin was a sign that you had to work outdoors and were therefore a labourer, poor and socially inferior. Pale white skin was admired instead as a sign of delicacy, prosperity and beauty.

The image we have in our minds of the perfect body may be culturally relative, but no matter: it is significant for us not because it is objectively 'true', but because it is universally held. It is an ideal we hold in common and to which we therefore aspire.

Of course very few people actually do look like this. The people in the newsagent looking at the magazines usually have embarrassing things like spots, not so gentle curves and wrinkly skin. At the more extreme end of the scale, obesity worries health officials more than most other health problems these days. Back in 1980, 14 per cent of Britons were seriously obese (30–40 lb over the recommended level). Today it is around 24 per cent. Within a generation, the figure could leap to as high as 40 per cent. Even if we look at those who are just 'overweight', two thirds of British men and over half of British women are simply too heavy. In the USA it is even worse: 127 million adults are overweight (that's more than 1 in 3), 60 million are obese and for around 9 million that condition is life threatening. In the USA about 28 per cent of pre-high-school children are obese, although the figure drops to 23 per cent at high-school age.[3] Nearly 28 per cent of British children aged between 2 and 10 are overweight and close to 14 per cent are obese.[4]

Those figures indicate a serious problem. They also tell us that there is a sizeable gap between the images of what the perfect body looks like and the reality most people experience. Even for those of us who don't have serious weight problems, our bodies are not as cooperative as we would like. They are gently voluptuous where they should be taut; podgy where they ought to be sleek. The images then begin to make us feel guilty. We stare enviously at the pictures, wishing we had bodies like that, bodies which we think would make us more sexually attractive, help us feel better about ourselves and increase our value in the eyes of others.

The gym and the promise

It is at that very point that the body-shaping industry kicks in. Our culture does not only hold up the image of the perfect body, it also puts in place the *means* by which we can get a body like those in the magazines. There exists a very large and lucrative mechanism that will relieve us of our cash to help us acquire such a body – from cosmetics, through workout programmes to plastic surgery. The quickest way to a six-pack is to get one fitted in a private hospital. The quickest way to lose weight is liposuction. Yet that is a bit extreme for most of us, even if we do want that smooth, muscled body. We go ahead and pick magazines from the shelves dedicated to showing us four easy ways to develop well-toned hips or a thinner waist. And most of all, we join a gym.

In fact, modern health and fitness centres lay out a classic narrative of salvation and damnation, a bit like a modern Pilgrim's Progress. The 'story' runs like this. Suppose you just eat as much as you like, whenever you like, and give up taking exercise (if you do any anyway). You keep on eating cake, chips, chocolate, sticky puddings and even deep fried Mars bars, while you slump in front of the TV, occasionally driving to your local pub where you down a few pints before rolling home to fall into bed. Sooner or later it begins to catch up on you. Your body starts to develop bulges, you can no longer fit into your old clothes (and have to spend money on new ones), and you look fat, unwieldy, bloated. You have to give up any idea of playing sport, begin to get out of breath when you climb stairs, and never manage to catch the bus when it is just leaving the stop. When you do have to run, you find yourself breathless, with your heart racing and your face as red as an apple. Before long, your heart begins to give out warning signs that all is not well. If not that, then diabetes, high blood pressure, high cholesterol, asthma or arthritis set in. You no longer attract the old admiring glances from the opposite sex, and your boyfriend or girlfriend begins to go off you, drawn to other slimmer, trimmer specimens. Your other friends begin to lose interest in this large slob they see developing in front of their eyes. You become a sad TV-ogling lump, with no other interests, unhealthy and unfit, with few friends and an empty life. This is the road to damnation.

The road to salvation runs in a different direction. You indulge a bit too much one Christmas. So, early in the New Year, you decide to join a gym. You pay your subscription, learn how to use the various appliances, start to exercise regularly and eat a more balanced diet. Your life begins to look up. You can do all kinds of things you couldn't do beforehand, like running up stairs, bending over without cricking your back, climbing over fences in the countryside without falling over. You start to take up sport and join a local tennis club. Your fitter, more healthy-looking frame begins to attract attention and you find yourself the object of admiring glances all round. Everyone wants to know you and you feel more confident, strong, healthy and fit. You are more alert thanks to your new regime of exercise and healthy eating, and you find yourself with more energy for work, leading to more success, promotion and more money. As you get older, you are able to defy the ageing process and still look and feel young. When many of your contemporaries are having heart attacks or strokes, you seem to go on for ever, playing golf into your eighties and playing energetically with your grandchildren. Life is full, and prospects for the future are good.

According to these stories, the key to health, success, prosperity, relationships and long life is good physical health and fitness. Just as much as any seventeenth-century reader might have recognized himself somewhere in John Bunyan's allegory, whether in the Slough of Despond or Vanity Fair, we recognize ourselves in this story of physical health and fitness.

So gyms are presented to us as a way not only of getting or remaining healthy, but also of sculpting the body we want to have (which is, in reality, the body we are told we want to have). As one advert for a local fitness centre put it: 'Get the body you want.'

Does gym fix it?

We know that to acquire such health, fitness or a finely sculpted body will cost something. It doesn't come cheaply, in money, time or effort. And people do it. To be serious about physical health and fitness requires a disciplined life. It requires a serious commitment to dieting, denying oneself certain kinds of food and adopting new habits of healthy eating and drinking. It demands time set aside for exercise which often feels painful and arduous. It needs a steeled will, to resist the temptation to stay in bed and instead to make it down to the gym for the aerobics class or the early morning swim. And it requires these things not in short bursts, followed by regular blowouts in between, but in sustained perseverance over many years.

We all know people, of course, who pay their gym subscription even though they hardly ever go. Of the 5 million new health club members each year, many never make it far beyond the front door or the coffee shop. They joined up in a fit of enthusiasm after a horrifying visit to the weighing scales one day, but never find the time or discipline to pursue that initial impulse. As one 40-year-old man put it, 'I find the idea of sitting on a stationary bike and watching MTV mind-numbingly boring . . . if I cancel, I know I won't go again. So although it's a bit mad to write the gym owner a free cheque every month, I'm keeping my options open.' Many like him don't do the exercises, but they do believe the myth.[5] And that is the point. Whether or not we actually do the exercises, we believe the story. We aspire and admire, even if we don't exercise. Gym offers a route to personal transformation, whether or not we take it.

By signing up for gym membership and paying a subscription, you can choose a personal fitness programme suited to your lifestyle. You can choose to work on your thighs, hips, biceps or six-pack, targeting effort on the areas where change is most needed. You can take classes at times that suit your lifestyle and work/home timetable, and round it all off with a healthy grape-fruit juice in the café afterwards with a friend who is working on a different area of their own body. And if you turn up to the classes, do the prescribed exercises and keep the discipline, then slowly, over time, you will change. Muscles will begin to appear, flab will begin to disappear. Your heart rate will decrease and you will find you are able to do things you could not do before – touch your toes, run upstairs without getting out of breath, or cope with stress a little better.

Gyms are places dedicated to the physical fitness of their members. Everything is tailored to enable people to 'work out' in whatever way they choose or feel they need, with a single clear goal in mind: to enable people to acquire physical health and

fitness, or to acquire the perfect body. It is the new asceticism. And it promises change.
Yet the desire for personal transformation goes beyond absorption with the body to a deepening interest in the soul.

Spiritual ideals

My local gym is simply called 'Spirit'. It is a strange name for an institution dedicated to physical rather than spiritual goals, but it is consciously tapping into a much wider phenomenon in contemporary culture that needs to be considered if we are to understand the way our society thinks about health and growth. As a recent article put it:

> Once religion formed the cornerstone of society. It gave us values to live by, a crutch to lean on, rituals to follow, mentors to guide us and communities to bond with. Today, our quest appears to be for a different and altogether more selfish kind of fulfilment: physical and emotional wellbeing.[6]

Alongside the desire for physical health and fitness goes a longing for something wider than the physical, which embraces other aspects of human experience as well. Many people today are searching not just for a physical solution to the stresses of the modern world, nor for a solely spiritual one, but for a more holistic path that encompasses body, mind and spirit. And that is why gyms like mine often position themselves as offering a wider sense of 'well-being' rather than just physical fitness.

This is a conscious rejection of many social and intellectual trends of the past few centuries. Various forms of idealism gave the impression that we are primarily minds in need of intellectual stimulation. Materialism in its various guises implied that we simply have physical needs that require satisfying. Spiritualized forms of religion thought we simply needed spiritual fulfilment, and should shun the needs of body and mind. Nowadays we are much more aware that we need a rounded solution that involves body, mind, spirit and emotions, if we are to find full health as human beings. The idea is to find a way of life that leads to physical, spiritual and emotional health, a balanced life that is useful, satisfying and fulfilling.

A year or two ago, around the corner from where I live, a restaurant opened where you could drink fruit juice or enjoy an organic salad meal, and then move on into the alternative therapy centre at the back of the building for a class on Tantric Yoga, Pilates or Zen meditation. Carrot juice and spirituality – a very twenty-first-century mix, precisely because it offers this union of spiritual and physical, a whole person approach.

It is a commonplace these days to point out the increasing interest in what is usually called 'spirituality'. This is usually accompanied by predictions of the demise of religion. For example, Paul Heelas and Linda Woodhead, in *The Spiritual Revolution: Why Religion Is Giving Way to Spirituality*, predict that within the next 20–30 years the subjective, inner-directed practices such as yoga, massage, meditation or aromatherapy will have eclipsed Christianity in the UK.[7] Yet, as they go on to comment, to have a narrow focus on 'spirituality' is actually to miss the point. People no more want a purely spiritual solution than they do a purely physical or mental one. The desire is for something more whole and all-encompassing.

On a recent transatlantic flight I was 'evangelized' by an employee of a company specializing in herbal remedies. In a classic sales pitch, after the normal general conversation about where we came from, families, destinations, etc., she began asking me whether I had ever tried alternative medicine. She showed me the catalogue and, as we were beginning the descent into Atlanta, moved in for the kill. Perhaps I wanted to order some tablets from their 'Thermojetics Program', some 'herbal concentrate' or even some 'Male Factor 1000', which apparently is a 'men's supplement for increased stamina and endurance'. Maybe she felt I needed some.

In a recent poll, 25 per cent of people sampled had tried complementary medicines of some kind of another, whether homeopathy, acupuncture, aromatherapy, reflexology or herbalism.[8] Many turn to alternative therapies because of a loss of faith in conventional medicine, and have found them invaluable in the management of pain and long-term illness. However, they also offer the same kind of restoration of balance, stimulation of parts of the body or soul normally left untouched, as more 'spiritual' types of therapy. One of the hallmarks of complementary medicine is a breaking down of the barriers between body and soul, realizing again that the two are interdependent. The rebellion against conventional medicine occurs precisely because in the past it has appeared to treat the body as a mechanism which bears little relation to the spiritual or psychological parts of human personality.

So the desire for physical health and fitness needs to be understood in the context of a wider sense of the need for holistic solutions. And gyms often present themselves in this very way. Yet it is at this point that a certain confusion enters the discussion.

The perfect soul?

Allan Bloom, in one of many perceptive comments in his provocative and powerful book *The Closing of the American Mind*, reflected on the goals of those he teaches in an American university. 'Students have powerful images of what a perfect body is, and pursue it incessantly. But . . . they no longer have any image of a perfect soul, and hence do not long to have one.'[9]

His comment reflects the contrast between a near unanimity on what our bodies are supposed to look like and a more confused picture when it comes to our inner life. The 'Mind, Body, Spirit' books or magazines often offer a sense of 'spiritual well-being', described with words such as 'fulfilment', 'peace', 'tranquillity', 'wholeness' or even, in more explicitly Buddhist language, 'enlightenment'. They offer a form of personal contentment that enables the searcher to deal with the stresses of twenty-first-century life. With a spiritually attuned 'centre', the devotee is meant to find an inner peace that will bring satisfaction or harmony.

Although there is a relational aspect to parts of the 'holistic spirituality' world, it is often presented in very personal, at times even narcissistic, terms. The goal in mind is that of the individual set apart, harmonized within him- or herself, brought to a state of inner tranquillity. From that state, he or she can manage all the stresses and pressures of modern life with a settled core of inner happiness and rest. The path laid out by the gym and the yoga class is actually very individualistic. Even if it does bring people into contact with each other, it still operates essentially as an individual vision which happens to bring like-minded people together to do such activities. The building of community does not seem to lie at the very heart of this vision of life.[10]

Most gyms are in fact not very communal. Clients work out on their exercise bikes or run on their treadmills, usually listening to their own choice of music through headphones, or looking with glazed eyes at either the ubiquitous TV set or the mirror that tells you how much sweat you're producing. Each person is locked into his or her own personal world, with individualized workout programmes and private space. Even the yoga class centres on individual meditative practices that can essentially be done alone. Other people are ultimately unnecessary. These may be a good way to build personal peace and tranquillity. They don't go very far towards building a strong sense of community.

Yet what does it really mean to be a 'perfect soul'? Is it the New Age vision of being in tune with the essential rhythms of mother earth? Is it 'reconnecting with our true selves', achieving serenity through meditation, giving up everything to work with the poor, or living the celebrity lifestyle? Allan Bloom is right – we have little consensus on what a 'perfect soul' looks like, so we search for it half-heartedly if we do so at all. Contrast that with our very clear image of the perfect body, and we can see why gyms are everywhere and make big money, while centres for spiritual healing or meditation still seem cranky and just a bit weird.

The church and the gym

However much Christians might look down their noses at the 'mind, body, spirit' phenomenon and the enthusiasm for joining health clubs, there is no doubt that for many people these routes do offer a path to genuine transformation. Gyms promise change. They fit into a coherent narrative which points out a way in which our lives will be better, richer, more fulfilling.

The contrast with church is stark. When asked to name an institution that offers a route to effective personal transformation, church would probably come pretty low on most people's lists. As one participant in the work conducted by Paul Heelas and Linda Woodhead put it, 'A one-hour service on a Sunday? It's not really enough time to address your self-esteem issues, is it? I didn't find any help in the churches. I found it in a 12-step programme. That was the start of my personal journey.' Church just did not seem to offer, let alone deliver, a path to personal transformation.

The verbs we use are significant. We speak of 'attending' church. The problem is that 'attending' is a static, passive activity. If you 'attend' something you just go to be there, not to be active or involved, not to learn or do something purposeful. We attend meetings, interviews, lectures. No one would speak of 'attending' the gym. Church has an image of being static, somewhere you go to sit, stand, sing, listen, and that's about it. It doesn't seem to promise personal change, and that perhaps is one of the main reasons why people don't choose to go.

Research carried out by Philip Richter and Leslie Francis into why people leave church found that, of those under 30 whom they interviewed, 37 per cent gave the reason for their departure as 'my church was no longer helping me to grow' (the figure was 23 per cent for those over 30). This was second only to 'I grew up and started making decisions on my own' (79 per cent and 42 per cent respectively), a factor which again suggests that churches have a lot of ground to make up in enabling people to grow into mature, holistic, responsible Christian faith and character.[11]

To many people, both inside and outside, church simply feels unnecessary. It seems irrelevant and self-referential, inducting people into its own rituals and practices, which bear little relation to life outside the walls.[12] It feels unnecessary because it doesn't seem to make any difference.

Chapter 1 made the point that such an image will not do the church any favours in a consumer culture. More than that, however, people are finding other avenues for changing their lives for the better, whether the key is felt to be physical or spiritual transformation. Church no longer has a monopoly on personal transformation, if it ever did. It is now in a competitive market, and it is losing out.

A new paradigm?

When Western societies were more explicitly Christian, the kind of discipline and effort now put into physical fitness went into the spiritual life. People tried to avoid the temptation to indolence and gluttony, and adopted disciplines such as prayer, fasting or frugality to ensure inner, spiritual purity and health. Today the need to avoid gluttony and the desire to live a frugal, simple life is just as common, but for different reasons. Gluttony is seen not so much as a spiritual danger but as a physical one. Frugality will provide an escape from the acquisitive rat race, not from the pains of hell. Overeating will threaten your life expectancy, not the state of your soul.

Although the growth of health clubs and centres of spiritual discovery might seem dangerous competition for the church, and therefore something to be opposed or feared, they may perhaps offer the church a vital clue as to where it is felt to be lacking. The gym 'story' might offer a model for how church could rediscover something more significant for the kind of people who go to gyms and are into 'spirituality'. It may even help it to rediscover some of its original calling, lost through the passage of time.

We saw earlier how the physical fitness industry works

because it has a clear story of salvation, progress and growth with which we can all identify. We also saw how there is little consensus on what a 'perfect soul' looks like. As it happens, this is one area where Christianity scores highly. It has a very clear idea of the 'perfect soul': it is portrayed for us in the person of Jesus Christ, the Word made flesh. Christian faith also has a distinct story, which describes us as made by a loving and infinitely creative God, set in a world of delight and wonder. It tells how our ancestors fell from grace, choosing the path of arrogance and disobedience rather than playing the divinely assigned role of stewards of the creation. It goes on to show how that act of disobedience was like a stone thrown into a pool, disturbing the clear, pure waters of the world with ripples which reach us today in the form of selfishness, pride, envy, jealousy, crime and death itself. It also offers a path of salvation – faith in Christ, the divine Word sent from the Father, lived out in a life of transformation through the Holy Spirit and renewed obedience, harmony and virtue, leading to participation in the new heaven and new earth which God will bring about one day.

It is a story that runs through the greatest literature, the finest art and architecture of the Western world over the past two millennia. It has a much longer and richer history than the story of salvation through physical fitness rehearsed earlier. Yet it connects with this story significantly.

At several points the New Testament uses the imagery of athletic contests and training as an image for growth in the life of Christ. Try these for example:

Train yourself to be godly. For physical training is of some value, but godliness has value for all things, holding promise for both the present life and the life to come.' (1 Tim. 4.7–8)

Run in such a way as to get the prize. Everyone who competes in the games goes into strict training. They do it to get a crown that will not last; but we do it to get a crown that will last for ever. Therefore I do not run like a man running aimlessly; I do not fight like a man beating the air. No, I beat my body and make it my slave so that after I have preached to others, I myself will not be disqualified for the prize. (1 Cor. 9.24–7)

Solid food is for the mature, who by constant use have trained themselves (the Greek word is *gymnazo* from which we get 'gymnasium') to distinguish good from evil. (Heb. 5.14)

In a culture that also prized athleticism, Paul was able to use physical training as an image for Christian growth and development. If this is a metaphor used by the earliest Christian writers, it may have some value for us. The gym might in fact prove a useful guide for the church in thinking about its role in twenty-first-century societies.

As we will see in later chapters, the church has a long and distinguished history in the arena of personal and spiritual transformation. The church has seen the acquisition of Christian character and virtue as a central goal of the Christian life. It has also tended to prescribe a series of spiritual disciplines, the practice of self-denial and an ordered life as the path to virtue and spiritual wholeness, all of this built upon a foundation of faith.

We sometimes think of our society as self-indulgent, narcissistic and extravagant. Discipline, self-denial, order and effort seem alien. Selling discipline or self-control to laid-back, private, twenty-first-century urban dwellers seems like selling top hats or penny-farthing bicycles: the need for such things went out a long time ago, and most of us feel we can survive very well without them now. Yet we understand perfectly the need for discipline in the area of physical and spiritual well-being. We all know that without such things as order and self-control we will never achieve the kind of physical and spiritual health we desire. This perhaps provides a clue to how the contemporary church can make significant connections for the kind of people we have been thinking about throughout this chapter.

The transformation from medicine balls, vaulting horses and old-fashioned PE to sleek health and fitness centres of today is not just the story of new decor, fancy design and sophisticated technology. It is also the story of the creation of a new narrative for people's lives and the promise of real personal transformation. It shows how exercise can make a profound difference – not just to your ability to play old-fashioned public school games, but also to work, relationships, sex, climbing stairs and longevity. Might there be a way in which theology, worship, church life and spiritual disciplines can all be recast so that they seem as vital and necessary to our spiritual well-being as exercise and healthy eating are to our physical state? Might there be a new way of capturing the imagination of our culture through offering a pathway to spiritual health and fitness that promises something far more deeply rooted and substantial than the vague, narcissistic offerings of the New Age? And might this vision actually help us return to what the church was always meant to be about?

Notes

1 See J. A. Mangan, *Athleticism in the Victorian and Edwardian Public School: The Emergence and Consolidation of an Educational Ideology*, New ed., *Sport in the Global Society*, 13 (London: Frank Cass, 2000); J. A. Mangan, *The Games Ethic and Imperialism: Aspects of the Diffusion of an Ideal*, Sport in the Global Society (London: Frank Cass, 1998).

2 See Alan Penn, *Targeting Schools: Drill, Militarism and Imperialism*, Woburn Education Series (London: Woburn, 1999).

3 Figures taken from the American Obesity Association: http://www.obesity.org/subs/fastfacts/aoafactsheets.shtml.

4 Figures from UK Department of Health: http://www.dh.gov.uk/Home/fs/en.

5 I'm using 'myth' in the technical sense as a story that embodies a truth, not as a 'falsehood'.

6 Claire Langham and Lucy Blakemore, 'Wellbeing: A New Religion?', *Admap*, June 2005.

7 Paul Heelas and Linda Woodhead, *The Spiritual Revolution: Why Religion Is Giving Way to Spirituality* (Oxford: Blackwell, 2005).

8 Poll of 1,001 UK adults carried out in December 2003 by *Populus*.

9   Allan Bloom, *The Closing of the American Mind* (New York: Simon & Schuster, 1987), p. 67.

10 Heelas and Woodhead point out the 'relationality' of the holistic milieu and how it operates in 'associational settings'. However, such interaction still seems secondary and does not lie at the heart of these practices. Around 20 per cent of their respondents indicated a relational aspect to their spiritual search. That still leaves 80 per cent who didn't! Heelas and Woodhead, *Spiritual Revolution*, p. 98f.

11 Philip Richter and Leslie J. Francis, *Gone but not Forgotten: Church Leaving and Returning* (London: DLT, 1998), p. 64.

12 One of the key findings in research on attitudes to church in contemporary society was precisely this sense that church was unnecessary and 'about itself'. See Nick Spencer and Graham Tomlin, *The Responsive Church* (Leicester: IVP, 2005), pp. 109–21.

Chapter 3

Spiritual health

Jacob Needleman is a professor of philosophy at San Francisco State University, a Jewish writer with a sympathetic interest in the Christian faith. In his book *Lost Christianity*, he examines a dissatisfaction he kept encountering among many Christians about their experience of their faith as it is expressed and practised in the modern world. He concluded that, compared to the normal experience of being a Christian today, in the early church there existed a more distinct and rigorous tradition of discipleship. Explaining the title of the book, he commented:

> . . . the lost element in Christianity is the specific methods and ideas that can, first, show us the subhuman level at which we actually exist, and, second, lead us towards the level at which the teachings of Christ can be followed in fact, rather than in imagination.[1]

His point is that something is missing in contemporary Christianity. Somehow churches have lost the ability to help people actually change in a profound and lasting way. As a result many people no longer care. Might this be recovered? If, as the last chapter suggested, the gym is a context in which many people today understand the need for physical growth and transformation, what might the Christian equivalent be? Churches don't focus on developing biceps and quads, but what do they develop?

Models of discipleship

When we think of Christian discipleship a number of possible models come to mind, and our model of discipleship is determined by what we consider to be the goal of Christian life. One such model is the 'academic' model. Here, maturity as a Christian is measured by how much you know about Christian theology or the Bible. The good Christian is one who can quote verses *and* tell you where they are found in the Bible. If this is the goal, then it is not surprising that Christian education or nurture primarily takes the form of lectures, sermons and the reading (and perhaps discussion) of books. In this model, every effort is made to get people to turn up to Christian teaching.

Another approach is what we might call the 'spirituality' model. Here, maturity is gauged by the quality of, or time spent in, prayer or meditation. Christian development consists of learning exercises in prayer, worship or contemplation. Yet another is what might be termed the 'social action' model. Here the goal is increased impact upon society, either through direct action or community projects. In this model, the mature disciple is one who signs up to and gets involved in a number of practical projects such as visiting the elderly, helping in drop-in centres for the homeless, or demonstrating in support of justice for the poor and oppressed.

Now all these have a vital role to play in Christian discipleship. Theology, prayer and practical action are all marks of true Christian life. Yet on their own they miss out something crucial, something which the New Testament stresses when it talks of the Christian life: the qualities of life which are expected to flow out of a Christian, or, to put it differently, the Christian virtues.

The climax of the letter written by Paul to the Christians in Galatia comes when he gives his list of the 'fruit of the Spirit'. The letter builds up its theology of the freedom that Christ has brought from the law. It then proceeds to argue that the purpose of that freedom is not licence but living by the Spirit. And the picture we are given of life in the Spirit comprises a certain list of qualities: 'love, joy, peace, patience, kindness, goodness, faithfulness, gentleness and self-control. Against such things there is no law' (Gal. 5.22–23). That is how we recognize true Christian life when we see it. We notice it by these very qualities or virtues, which undergird and are expressed in everything else. Faith is the foundation of the Christian life, but if you are a Christian you are also meant to:

> . . . add to your faith goodness; and to goodness, knowledge; and to knowledge, self-control; and to self-control, perseverance; and to perseverance, godliness; and to godliness, brotherly kindness; and to brotherly kindness, love. For if you possess these qualities in increasing measure, they will keep you from being ineffective and unproductive in your knowledge of our Lord Jesus Christ. (2 Pet. 1.5–8)

New Testament authors are not casuists. When they write about the Christian life, they do not tend to lay down detailed instructions on what to do in certain circumstances. There isn't a lot of 'law' in the New Testament, if law is understood as a body of instruction that covers all eventualities and gives you guidelines on every possible moral conundrum which might come up. It does have some of that – there are some clear guidelines about what we are and are not to do with our money, our sexuality or our neighbours. Yet more often than not, however, the epistles end up with something like this:

> Pursue righteousness, godliness, faith, love, endurance and gentleness. (1 Tim. 6.11)

> I urge . . . you to live a life worthy of the calling you have received. Be completely humble and gentle; be patient, bearing with one another in love. Make every effort to keep the unity of the Spirit through the bond of peace (Eph. 4.1–3)

> Therefore, as God's chosen people, holy and dearly loved, clothe yourselves with compassion, kindness, humility, gentleness and patience. Bear with each other and forgive whatever grievances you may have against one another. Forgive as the Lord forgave you. (Col. 3.12–13)

In other words, the New Testament urges the cultivation of certain qualities of life as the true indicator of Christian maturity. If these qualities are noticeable in a Christian's life he is effective and fruitful; if not, he is not effective or fruitful, however much he knows about theology or marches for justice. But how are such things to be cultivated in busy, contemporary Christian lives?

Spiritual fitness and the virtues

As I mentioned in the introduction, a new gym recently opened in our area. Curious, I strolled along to take a look. A leaflet advertised a menu of exercise programmes. I could sign up for a class that would help me develop a flat stomach. I could go to another that would work on toning my thighs. Yet another aimed to strengthen weak backs and another promised better posture.

In a brightly lit room, a large number of sweaty people were pounding away on exercise cycles, treadmills, weights and pulleys. The machines did bear some resemblance to instruments of medieval torture, yet these people had actually paid to go on them, so they can't have been that bad. Looking more closely, I realized that each machine was meant to help you work on a different part of your body – legs, abdomen, biceps, shoulders or pectorals.

Here was a place where you could focus on the specific parts of your body that were either weak or underdeveloped. The parallels began to form in my mind. We spend vast amounts of time, money and effort developing physical fitness. What would it mean to cultivate *spiritual* fitness? What would it take to develop certain parts of the spiritual life, virtues of character and action, just as we try to develop certain parts of our bodies?

The US President's Council on Physical Fitness and Sports says, 'Physical fitness is to the human body what fine-tuning is to an engine. It enables us to perform up to our potential.' We acquire it by exercising our bodies to bring out muscles that lie undeveloped and to encourage the different organs of the body to work efficiently and effectively. It means becoming more of the person we can be, at least in physical terms.

Spiritual fitness is much the same in another sphere. Rather than improving muscle strength or body tone, it means developing spiritual qualities which enable you to do things that might otherwise be beyond you. It means developing qualities of love, patience, generosity, forgiveness, grace, and so on. These qualities are the very ones that will enable you to keep a marriage together, give generously to those who need it even when you're short of cash, react with grace and kindness to someone who offends you, or remain patient with an infuriating and unfair colleague at work or in church.

A spiritually fit person might or might not be physically fit or healthy, but he or she will have developed the qualities of love, generosity, forgiveness and kindness. In short, such a person will have developed virtue.

Virtue and character

An important distinction needs to be made here. There is a great difference between a generous act and a generous person, or a courageous act and a courageous person. Most people are capable of a generous act from time to time, by a supreme effort of will. But that is very different from having generosity built into the very fabric and tenor of a life. An example used by C. S. Lewis might help. Even bad tennis players can play good shots occasionally. By fluke or out of a modicum of skill, there are quite a few people who can pull a backhand top-spin cross-court winner out of the bag every now and again. It is very different to be able to do it regularly, almost as a matter of course. The average player might pull it off once in ten tries; a good player will do it more often than not; an excellent player will do it nine times out of ten. Moreover, the average player will regularly hit easy shots long or into the net, whereas the good player will play these without any trouble time and time again. As Lewis explains:

What you mean by a good player is a man whose eye and muscles and nerves have been so trained by making innumerable good shots that they can now be relied on . . . Now it is that quality rather than the particular actions which we mean when we talk of a 'virtue'.[2]

When we talk about Christian virtue, what we mean is a particular quality of life that regularly issues in particular kinds of actions. The focus is not so much on the actions themselves, but on the quality of life that makes them possible. This is why physical fitness is a useful image for us. A fit person may be able to run up stairs nimbly and quickly, but that is not because she has learnt the specific bodily movements needed to run up stairs; it is simply because she is generally fit. She has developed a quality in her body that enables it to do that kind of thing. A mature Christian is someone in whom a quality of life has grown that enables her to be generous even when she is poor, to love until it hurts, to show kindness as a regular habit of life, without even thinking about it.

This is the bit that is often hard to grasp. There is a tradition of Christian moral thought that sees discipleship solely as obedience. There is real value in this, and it is certainly an idea that the New Testament supports, but it can lead in unfortunate directions. It can imply that Christian behaviour is simply a matter of obeying certain rules or laws. In each individual choice or action, it can suggest that we are, as it were, to consult the divine instruction manual and carry out the required action because it says so. Yet as we know so well, it is quite possible to be an obedient person but have a rebellious heart. Many a child obeys the stern parent because he knows there is not much option, yet underneath he is seething with resentment. Many adults can be obedient to what they think is expected of them, but their heart remains sluggish, reluctant and unengaged with the process. That kind of conformity is not what God wants from us, nor is it good for us. Obedience that constantly cuts across our wills eventually leads to bitterness and unresolved frustration. The true end of Christian nurture is not to force an unwilling obedience out of a rebellious heart, but to change the heart so that it results in glad, willing obedience.

Very often we hear calls to return to 'Christian standards' or 'Christian values' in social life. The idea seems to be that if only we could restore some kind of consensus on what people ought to do, then somehow the world would be a whole lot better. Or alternatively, we are called to act on the basis of Christian 'principles', conveying the idea that Christian behaviour consists of working out some basic rules from the Bible or some other source, and then acting according to them in specific moral cases.

These approaches may have merits as far as they go, but they miss something vital. It is one thing to work out what you should do; it is another to enable people to do it. Christian faith is a lot more than a set of rules to govern society. It is quite possible for everyone to agree on the rules, yet to find few people actually capable of obeying them. The point of the new covenant as the prophets saw it was not that God would give us a new law, but that the law would be written on our hearts:

> I will give you a new heart and put a new spirit in you;
> I will remove from you your heart of stone and give you a
> heart of flesh. And I will put my Spirit in you and move
> you to follow my decrees and be careful to keep my laws.
> (Ezek. 36.26–27)

The new covenant changes our ability to obey the law by placing something new within our hearts, so that it becomes natural, almost easy, to obey, just as it is natural or easy for a physically fit person to run for a bus or lift a heavy box without permanent damage, or for the leader of my Pilates class to walk with a balance and poise of which I could only dream.

God's desire is for changed hearts, not merely outward actions. It is not that he is unconcerned for actions and only cares about the inner life. It is more that the kind of actions he likes are those that come from the heart. They are the kind of actions that, in a sense, a person doesn't even have to think about – the heart has become so warmed, changed and practised in certain attitudes that it produces these actions automatically, as a matter of course. It is about becoming the kind of person who tends to act generously, kindly, graciously, rather than someone who just occasionally is able to perform a merciful act.

Virtue ethics

In the past few decades there has been a significant growth in interest in this way of thinking about the moral life, and not just in Christian circles.[3] 'Virtue ethics' has developed as a way of thinking about morality that on the whole questions the idea of 'duty'.

A seminal book on this theme was Alasdair MacIntyre's *After Virtue*, which appeared in 1985. MacIntyre highlighted what he considered to be a crisis in moral thinking since the Enlightenment of the eighteenth century. On the one hand, Immanuel Kant, alongside Hume, Diderot and other Enlightenment moralists embraced a vision of the moral life as obedience to a set of rules or principles which were derived not so much directly from God, but from within human experience. At the same time, the Enlightenment did away with any overarching sense of purpose in human life. There was no conception that humanity had any kind of ideal to strive for, or model to follow. Teleology, or the notion of purpose or goal, was shunned – there was no divine image to be restored, nor was there any sense of moral progress by which we are to become something other than what we already are.

The difficulty, as MacIntyre pointed out, was that these two aspects of Enlightenment ethics don't fit together well. How can you have rules if you don't know what they are for? We know how a cello should and should not be treated, because we know what its purpose is. It exists to make sweet-sounding music, so caring for it gently, keeping it in a solid case and sweeping a taut bow across its strings are all right and proper. Using it to sit on or to fry an egg would be disastrous, because it doesn't fit with the purpose for which it was made. The attempt to build a morality without a sense of human purpose was bound to fail: 'Moral judgments are linguistic survivals from the practices of classical theism which have lost the context provided by these practices.'[4]

The approach MacIntyre suggests, a return to the notion of virtue, doesn't focus on an obligation to obey the will of God, or the self-imposed duty to obey the 'categorical imperatives' foundational in Kant's thinking on the moral life. It also rejects the utilitarian approach as developed, for example, by John Stuart Mill, who argued that 'actions are right in proportion as they tend to promote happiness, wrong as they tend to produce the reverse of happiness'.[5] Such ideas are jointly problematic, as they both impose morality on us from the outside, regardless of whether our inner heart or soul wants to follow.

Virtue ethics, as this approach has been called, also questions the idea of the moral life as simply acting on certain 'principles' that are meant to govern behaviour. One difficulty with 'principles' is how useful they are in the face of complex moral dilemmas. They are helpful as far as they go, but are sometimes too abstract and general to help in sorting out complex moral questions. For example, 'just war' theory may be valid, but what happens when no one can quite agree on whether a particular conflict passes the test or not? The principle of justice for the poor is another example: how exactly is that to be achieved in the complex realities of international economics?

In any case, virtue ethicists argue that to become good, it is not enough just to apply certain principles. Instead, they say that the key questions in ethics are actually about human character. We need not so much to establish a set of abstract principles as to cultivate the kind of character that will act wisely and justly in different situations – a bit like developing the skill to hit a good tennis shot, whatever angle or speed the ball may be hit towards you. At the very least, an ethics of principles needs to be supplemented by an ethics of virtue.

The good or virtuous person acts not out of concern for the maximization of the good (Mill) or adherence to law or duty (Kant), but out of a quality of virtue that has been developed through a lifetime of experience and practice. Virtues are learnt in the same way in which we mostly learn to play football, dance, carve wood or cook – through example and imitation, not logic and principles. We watch those who are already good at these things, experience a desire to be like them, and so we start to copy them. A person of virtue does not have to think too hard about doing the right thing; he or she will do it naturally, without thinking. A good tennis player will not consciously work out the angles in her head, define the shot she needs to play, then execute the stroke – she will just play the right shot instinctively, hardly thinking at all.

This debate between 'duty ethics' and 'virtue ethics' has often been portrayed as an argument between Kant and Aristotle, chief figures in two different strands of ethical thought. As it happens, they are probably not as opposed as is sometimes thought. Aristotle does have some notion of duty and morality, and Kant has an idea of virtue. The polarity is dangerous if pushed too hard. Each needs the other. However, the idea of prioritizing virtue over duty helps us to think about the person who is acting, about what kind of person they are, and not only about whether the actions themselves are objectively right or wrong. It also helps us to think less about external adherence to rules and more about the heart – a key concern for Christian thinking about discipleship and behaviour.

The other key point MacIntyre makes is that essential to the cultivation of virtue is the telling of stories. In ancient cultures you knew who you were because you knew your place in these stories. Homer's great poems were recited as a public event, telling the history of the city and its heroes. Icelandic sagas had the same purpose. The stories told you who you were and how you fitted into the world. The past had bequeathed a specific order to the present, usually based around family kinship or the civic or household hierarchy.[6] Such people were unable to think of themselves outside their own stories or histories – they defined who they were and left them in no doubt as to their proper place in the world.

MacIntyre points out that we are all defined by the stories we believe about who we are and where we came from, and those stories are different. Moreover, the only way virtues can be developed or even conceived is by reference to those stories. If you live in a society which has always survived by hunting, then skill at throwing spears or shooting arrows, or even an ability to go for days without food yourself in order to secure the kill which will feed the tribe for a week, are the virtues you strive for. If you live in a culture which prizes the eloquence of the poet as the one who reminds the community of its past, then skill in spinning a good story (one which is true to the community's traditions and past history) will be the desired virtue.

Today, however, we value the ability to distance ourselves from our own culture or history. We are all taught to stand autonomously outside our own tradition and history and to critique it, question it and even to think we live outside 'stories' altogether. And that gives us a problem when it comes to virtue: we don't really know what we want. This is where Christian moral and spiritual thinking comes in.

Christian virtue ethics
Virtue ethics usually looks back to Aristotle as its originator, but he was not a Christian. McIntyre, although himself a Christian, based his approach on Aristotle's moral scheme. For him, a return to virtue was a return to Aristotle. Later (especially Christian) writers have taken him to task on this, John Milbank, for example, arguing that a more properly Christian approach would take a different route and that we need a more thoroughly Christian basis for thinking about virtue.[7] He shows how Greek notions of character are indelibly bound up with the heroic model and defence of the city. Achilles, Ajax and Ulysses may be heroes in battle, but they are still killers. Their virtues are the qualities that help them win wars and defend honour, such as cunning and pride. They also have (at least from other ethical perspectives) deep moral flaws: Achilles is petulant and arrogant, Ajax jealous and uncontrolled, Ulysses vengeful and violent.

Christian behaviour, as Milbank points out, is based not on conflict but on love, because God is love. Christian virtues are those required to live together in harmony and peace, not to win battles; while they overlap with the classic Greek virtues, they are different.

For Aristotle, humility is not a virtue, but pride is (for example, pride in your own or your city's honour). Humility was an appropriate attitude before the gods, but certainly not recommended in your relationships with other people. In the New Testament humility is a virtue, pride a sin. Again, love for an enemy or someone of inferior status was highly prized in the culture of the earliest churches. It was shameful in wider Greco-Roman culture. So the New Testament's instruction to 'do nothing out of selfish ambition or vain conceit, but in humility consider others better than yourselves' (Phil. 2.3) would have sounded very strange indeed. Forgiveness and charity are absent from Aristotle's list of the virtues. In fact, as MacIntyre points out, Aristotle would not have especially admired either Jesus or Paul, had he met them.

Virtue and the church

One other prominent Christian writer who has given much thought to the idea of virtue is the American theologian Stanley Hauerwas. 'Any community or polity', he argues, 'is known and should be judged by the kind of people it develops.'[8] Those outside the church are perfectly within their rights to look at the church and judge it on the quality of life they see emerging from it. For Hauerwas, the development of virtue is the central task of the church, more important than having an impact on society or influencing culture to make it more Christian. Christians have no interest in the business of shoring up a society that does not try to live by the gospel. The attempt to influence culture, to make society more just, fair or simply a bit more Christian is doomed to failure. The whole project of liberal societies is to try to 'create just societies without just people'.[9] He also argues that just people cannot be produced, as we will see, by a society with no common story, no shared history.

That does not mean, however, that the church has to become a private sect, completely cut off from or ignoring the existence of the world around it. The church is political not in the sense that it has to try its hardest to make the world a better place, but in the sense that it shows the world what it really is – created by God for human community in fellowship with God. It does that by being itself, not taking its cue from the values of the surrounding culture and trying to ape that with a religious tinge to it, but adopting a different way, marked particularly in Hauerwas's view by the refusal to resort to violence or coercion to achieve its ends.

So, Hauerwas argues, 'the most important social task of Christians is to be nothing less than a community capable of forming people with virtues sufficient to witness to God's truth in the world'.[10] The church has something to say to the world, but only by being thoroughly and stubbornly itself. Only when the church learns to be properly independent, governed by its own doctrine and polity, can it really be of any use within the world, because only then will it be able to offer real transformation and real virtue. 'Insofar as the church can reclaim its integrity as a community of virtue, it can be of great service in liberal societies.'[11] In fact, 'The most important service the church does for any society is to be a community capable of developing people of virtue.'[12]

The particular contribution Hauerwas brings to this debate, then, is an appreciation of the role of the church in the cultivation of virtue, not just for its own sake but for the sake of the world itself. For Hauerwas, 'Christian beliefs only make sense when embodied in a political community we call church.'[13] It is only by becoming part of the church and learning its particular way of life and practices that Christian faith and doctrine begin to make sense. It is reminiscent of Augustine's notion that only by loving God can we come to know him: a purely distant, academic understanding will never be enough. Growing in Christian spiritual health, unlike the pursuit of physical fitness, is essentially communal. Not only does it lead to qualities that enable people to live together despite their differences, it is also learnt in community. We will explore this theme more fully later on.

Friends and families

The other key aspect of the church is that we do not choose its members. One of the classic TV programmes of the past decade has been the wonderfully funny and inventive *Friends*, which ran from 1994 to 2004. Not only was it brilliantly written, it was also fascinating social history. Previously, sitcoms typically featured families – usually father, mother and various kids. *Friends* announced the end of the family, or at least replaced it with a new unit of social life: flatmates. The families of Rachel, Phoebe, Monica, Ross, Chandler and Joey were in the background to emerge at various moments for comic effect, but largely they were secondary characters to the main six, whose bonds were not those of family but of friendship.[14]

We choose our friends, but we are stuck with our families. The characters of *Friends* are all young and good looking. They are all white, middle class, from similar social backgrounds, and they are drawn together by the simple fact that they like each other – that's what friends are. With families, despite genetic likenesses, it seems much more random. In a moment of frustration, one of Douglas Coupland's characters in *Generation X* says:

> I really think that when God puts together families he sticks
> his finger into the white pages and selects a group of
> people at random, and says to them all, 'Hey, you're going
> to spend the next 70 years together, even though you have
> nothing in common, and don't even like each other. And,
> should you not feel yourself caring about this group of
> strangers even for a second, you will feel just dreadful.'[15]

Yet with families it is precisely this randomness that makes them such formative communities. Families are places where we learn to love those who are different from us, whose friendship we would not necessarily choose. In families people who are plain, awkward and unattractive can find acceptance and belonging. They are special, just because they are a son, daughter, father or mother. If a friend becomes gradually less attractive or fun to be with, we may drift apart. With families we have to work harder at it. Families are more difficult, but more rewarding. That is why families have more potential to mould, shape and change us, to teach us to love those who are unlike us, than friendships (but only if we stick with them). It may also explain why the Bible uses the metaphor of family more often than that of friendship to describe the church.

Church is like family precisely because we don't choose our fellow Christians. Family is the place where we learn to love those we do not choose to love.[16] It is the school in which we are formed in the particular glory of being human – the ability to love those who are unlike us. The same is true of church. Just as families are small communities in which we learn skills we would otherwise not develop, churches, precisely because they put us with people we would not have chosen for ourselves, give us the context in which we can develop virtue and character. Families teach us the virtues those particular people prize. I love God, books and football largely because my father did. He never sat me down and told me that's what I should do; I just picked it up. That was the story of my family, the things that were valued there. In church we learn a particular set of virtues that come out of the story of the Bible, which we read day after day, week after week.

Discipleship is about the development of Christian character. It involves the ability to do the will of God without really thinking about it – in a sense, without effort. Christian virtues are only developed in relationship with other Christians; in other words, in church. Yet if our churches are to take this task seriously, they may have to look quite different from the way they do at present. The challenge is to enable churches to be every bit as dedicated to the goal of spiritual health and fitness, the cultivation of Christian virtues, as gyms are to the development of physical health and fitness. That is a real challenge. Yet this task is vital, not just for the survival of the church, but perhaps even for the survival of our culture and even the planet on which we live. The next chapter explores why.

Notes

1   Jacob Needleman, *Lost Christianity* (Shaftesbury: Element, 1993), p. 155.
2   C. S. Lewis, *Mere Christianity* (London: Fount, 1997), p. 66.
3   For an introduction to this see Daniel Statman, 'Introduction to Virtue Ethics', in *Virtue Ethics*, Daniel Statman, ed. (Edinburgh: Edinburgh University Press, 1997).
4   Alasdair MacIntyre, *After Virtue: A Study in Moral Theory*, 2nd ed. (London: Duckworth, 1985), p. 60.
5   From Mill's essay 'Utilitarianism', in John Stuart Mill, *On Liberty and Other Essays*, *Oxford World's Classics* (Oxford: OUP, 1998), p. 137.
6   MacIntyre, *After Virtue*, pp. 121–3.
7   John Milbank, *Theology and Social Theory: Beyond Secular Reason*, *Signposts in Theology* (Oxford: Blackwell, 1990). To be fair to MacIntyre, he does acknowledge the difference between Greek and Christian ideas of virtue – see chapters 13 and 14 of *After Virtue*. He does, however, continue to think primarily of a return to Aristotle, whereas Milbank sees the need for a return to a more distinctively Christian vision of the moral life based on Augustine.
8   Stanley Hauerwas, *A Community of Character: Toward a Constructive Christian Social Ethic* (Notre Dame: University of Notre Dame, 1981), pp. 2, 51.
9   Stanley Hauerwas and Charles Pinches, *Christians among the Virtues: Theological Conversations with Ancient and Modern Ethics* (Notre Dame: University of Notre Dame, 1997), p. 149.
10   Hauerwas, *Community of Character*, p. 3.
11   Stanley Hauerwas, *Vision and Virtue: Essays in Christian Ethical Reflection* (Notre Dame: University of Notre Dame, 1981), p. 7.
12   *Ibid.*, p. 13.
13   Stanley Hauerwas, *After Christendom?: How the Church Is to Behave if Freedom, Justice, and a Christian Nation Are Bad Ideas*, 2nd ed. (Nashville: Abingdon Press, 1999), p. 26.
14   In case *Friends* fanatics spot the flaw in this, yes of course Ross and Monica are brother and sister, but they might as well not be for the primary purposes of most of the comedy. Their family relationship is played on at times, but is usually secondary to the main storylines.
15   Douglas Coupland, *Generation X: Tales for an Accelerated Culture* (London: Abacus, 1992), p. 36.
16   See Hauerwas, *Community of Character*, chapter 8.

Chapter 4

Culture and character

How do you get people to behave? Everyone who has ever taken up any position of leadership has asked that question. Whether it is a teacher faced with a rowdy class, an employer dealing with a demotivated workforce or a politician attempting to solve problems such as violent crime or marital breakdown, they have all tried to find ways of cultivating the kind of behaviour that will make their communities work better.

The question of behaviour is the other side of the quest for personal fulfilment we have been considering. The individual is looking for a way of life that will bring spiritual and physical well-being, contentment, positive relationships and satisfaction. Politicians and community leaders have an interest in something similar. They want to build functioning, cohesive communities. They want people to develop healthy relationships, a sense of self-worth and basic contentment with life, because such people tend to contribute towards building a healthy society. Angry, discontented people with low self-worth and a chip on their shoulder will destroy rather than build community.

So the question of personal transformation and how it is achieved is more than a privatized pursuit of the affluent. It has a far wider social significance. Our societies have a real interest in developing people who can remain honest in business, keep families together, restrain and channel their anger wisely and behave civilly and generously to their neighbours.

Yet we have a problem. Our culture has a deep aversion to being told what to do. We don't like 'morality'. Whenever political, community or religious leaders try to tell people how to behave, we start talking about the 'nanny state' or 'self-appointed moral guardians'. The fact that 'laying down the law' has become a pejorative term says everything about our attitude to moral instruction.

Allan Bloom starts his trenchant critique of contemporary popular intellectual culture, *The Closing of the American Mind*, with the statement, 'There is one thing a professor can be absolutely certain of: almost every student entering the university believes, or says he believes, that truth is relative.'[1] As a result, such students also believe that no particular moral code can be imposed upon anyone, because no set of rules can claim objective ultimate truth. We are free moral agents, at liberty to make up our own rules, our own codes of behaviour and no external authority has the right to infringe the liberty of the individual by telling us what to do. We may well be free to pursue our own path of spiritual, physical and emotional well-being, but that very individualistic vision of life doesn't sit easily with our need to find a common set of values to live by, one that might have a chance of holding our societies together, with all their ethnic, economic and social diversity.

The roots of autonomy

All of this has deep roots in cultural shifts that have taken place over the past few hundred years. Medieval Europe was a place where the rules of society or religion dominated life. In such a hierarchical society most people knew their place in the pecking order, and they had to act in a way that fitted that place, obeying their 'lord' or whoever was a rung higher up the social ladder. The medieval church developed an extensive code of canon law to order life. The church regulated disputes between neighbours, monasteries or businesses, all based on the law of God revealed in the Bible, and taught by the theologians of the church.

During the Enlightenment of the seventeenth and eighteenth centuries, however, the infallibility of God's law revealed in the Bible and controlled by the church was radically questioned. The discovery of other, non-Western cultures with their own systems of law and order inevitably raised the question of the universality of biblical law. The religious wars of the seventeenth century taught Europeans a further lesson: how can we be expected to bow to the rules of the church when the church itself can't make up its mind what the rules are?

A new way of thinking about the basis of moral action had to come about, and one of its main architects was a philosopher we touched on in the last chapter, Immanuel Kant (1724–1804). Kant claimed that our knowledge of the world is filtered and shaped by our own subjective experience of it. This includes morality. Access to some divine law just handed to us on a plate will not work. Instead, he wanted to find a form of ethics independent of religion or tradition – something that could be validated by human experience, which is all we can be sure of. He argued that humans are to act according to 'categorical imperatives', rational principles valid under all circumstances and to be followed at all times. We should act only in ways that can be shown to be applicable in all circumstances. For him, the basic rule of ethics was: 'I should never act except in such a way that I can also will that my maxim should become a universal law.'[2]

These maxims are established not by God or any past tradition, but by our own will. In fact for Kant, 'autonomy of the will' is the supreme principle of morality and 'heteronomy of the will' (rules imposed from the outside) is the source of all errors in ethics.[3] So, according to Kant, morality is established by and aligns with our own will: 'All maxims are rejected which are not consistent with the will's own legislation of universal law.'[4] The result was a moral system that took away God as the central authority in telling us what we should or shouldn't do, but it still had *duty* built firmly into its foundations.

Kant was writing in the context of the Enlightenment project that tried to replace reliance on revelation with dependence on human reason to establish truth. The great fear in this was that once you took away God, might moral chaos then ensue? Kant, however, showed that you do not necessarily need God to uphold the moral fabric of society. Kant believed in God, but he derived a system of ethics without recourse to heteronomy (literally 'another law'). His version of morality was subjective, in that it derives from the human will, but also objective, in that by adopting only maxims that could be more widely applicable, you could find binding rules for everyone. Contemporary popular morality has taken Kant's dislike of imposed rules from outside very much to heart. But it has also turned against any substantial sense of wider moral duty, whether established by God, church, aristocracy or white middle-class males like Immanuel Kant. It is not only God's laws we feel free to disagree with, but also those of anyone who tries to tell us what we should or shouldn't do. If there remains a sense of duty, it is now merely duty to oneself, the imperative to 'be myself', the law of personal self-realization. Polonius's pompous and somewhat fatuous advice to Laertes in Shakespeare's *Hamlet*, 'This above all: to thine own self be true', has been taken as the central moral principle of a generation. Or, in the words of that other great philosopher Dolly Parton, 'Find out who you are, then do it on purpose.'

Yet how do you harmonize an ultimate duty to 'be yourself' with the need for society to function well? If my only duty is to be true to myself, can that really build community? What if my path to fulfilment conflicts with someone else's? Individuals search for personal harmony, politicians look for social harmony, but can the two coincide in a culture where there is an inbuilt suspicion of heteronomous law? The basic problem is that we need to find a way of living together, but don't like anyone imposing laws or rules on us.

Problems in paradise

The problem hits home more deeply than at the level of ideas. Although the Enlightenment (and Kant's own) writings were liberally sprinkled with predictions that human social and intellectual problems were on the verge of being solved, that eighteenth-century confidence sounds quite hollow at the start of the twenty-first. We still sense the need for some kind of renewal of life and behaviour. The autonomy of the individual may enable us to pursue our own version of personal well-being, but it can also lead to less welcome outcomes: statistics concerning teenage pregnancies, school discipline, divorce, binge drinking, drug taking and child abuse remain much too high for comfort in most Western societies, even where they are not actually increasing.

Programmes for change

Finding the answer to such problems is no easy matter. In fact, deep divides run through political opinion on the proper solution. For those on the right, the answer lies in a return to traditional morality, strict rules enforced by strengthened social control. More disciplinary powers should be given to figures of authority such as teachers, parents and police officers; manners, respect and morality should be taught by politicians, schools and churches. For others on the left, authority figures such as the police are part of the problem, not the solution, and need to be made properly accountable. The problem is not the lack of external authority – that only creates sullen, unwilling compliance, exacerbates social tension and maintains unjust social structures. Instead, the problem lies more with the social conditions in which people have to live. The provision of better social facilities, the alleviation of poverty and the removal of oppressive assumptions that confine and repress minority groups are the ways forward. These two options are, of course, polarized and caricatured. Many would suggest some kind of combination of the two – greater powers to the police along with better social provision and justice. However, the two approaches do draw attention to real confusion over how some of the deep-seated social problems of our time can be overcome. The split between left and right is itself deeply damaging and leads to a greater sense of instability, especially in a culture like that of the USA, where the chasm runs more deeply through political and social life than it does in Europe.

Both sides admit there is a problem, and from time to time politicians have tried to come up with answers. Back in 1993, John Major's UK government launched a 'Back to Basics' campaign, with the prime minister announcing, 'It is time to get back to basics: to self-discipline and respect for the law, to consideration for others, to accepting responsibility for yourself and your family, and not shuffling it off on the state.' Rightly or wrongly, the campaign led to intense interest in the private lives of Major's cabinet ministers and, perhaps not surprisingly, uncovered a whole raft of scandals that fatally undermined the credibility of the project. The venture fell victim to the same trend we have been discussing – the dislike of being told what to do, especially by a group of people who didn't seem to set much store by these 'basics' in their own private lives. 'Back to Basics' was soon abandoned. A moral crusade had failed due to the fragility of personal character.

In 2005 the newly elected third-term government of Tony Blair announced a series of measures under the heading of restoring 'Respect' to society. Concerned about levels of crime, disorder and particularly violence and binge drinking endemic in parts of British urban youth culture, the government launched another attempt to instil values of mutual concern and recognition in social relationships. As we have seen, however, that is hard to do in a culture of aggressive individualism, a culture which many commentators suggest has been fostered rather than inhibited by both Thatcherism and the New Labour project.

Basically, such campaigns lack credibility. The dilemma is that while, on the one hand, we dislike external rules and value personal autonomy, on the other hand, we also dislike the results of a society based on individual choice, and a lack of moral consensus. We like our individualism, yet we dislike the resulting lack of communality.

The problem lies beyond the scope of politics. There are deep-rooted ambivalences and contradictions in our social fabric. We need to take another approach, which is to start looking at how we help people develop the impulses to behave well towards each other. We need to explore the idea of 'character'.

Undermining character

Character is different from personality. 'Personality' describes particular characteristics that make us distinct from one another. When we describe someone as having an extrovert personality, being shy or thoughtful, these are morally neutral and do not imply any sense of judgement. These are usually things over which we have little control, aspects of ourselves which we were born with or have developed from an early age. 'Character', however, describes features which do have moral value and over which we have a measure of control as we develop. The notion of character contains such qualities as faithfulness, reliability, honesty or kindness. We don't really mind if our neighbours are gregarious or diffident. We do mind if they are inconsiderate or deceitful. The former can be described as aspects of personality, the latter aspects of character.

The sociologist Richard Sennett has given serious thought to the effects of modern social trends upon the notion of character. His book *The Corrosion of Character* is a perceptive and eye-opening study of the effect modern working practices have upon people caught up in the race to succeed.[5] The flexible marketplace means that young people embarking on a career can no longer expect their working life to be spent entirely within the same profession, let alone the same company. Nor would they wish it to happen – staying in the same job for decades on end is now a sign not of dependability or constancy, but of a lack of ambition. Young Americans leaving college can now expect to change jobs an average of eleven times during their career, and their entire skill base around three times.[6] The problem is that this flexibility commonly erodes certain qualities that are vital for the health of society – trustworthiness, commitment, purpose and loyalty. To be always ready to change tack at any point, to jump ship from one company, career or marriage to another means deliberately avoiding long-term commitments, sitting loose to colleagues and projects, a string of shallow relationships and constant uncertainty.

Jobs now tend not to build up a unique skill or craft, acquired over a lifetime, such as the knowledge of how to bake bread, make shoes or carve furniture. Instead workers are more likely to supervise a computerized system for making the soles of a particular type of footwear, or be responsible for packaging the sections of a flat-pack wardrobe, rather than learning how to make the wardrobe from scratch. This lacks any sense of the long-term task of struggling to master a fully rounded skill or trade, or the art of self-discipline in the use of working time – some of the features of life that can build self-esteem, proper pride in work well done and a sense of self-respect. In fact, skills and experience built up over a long period of time are now valued less than the capacity to let go of such experience to switch work pathways at the drop of a hat. Even though the popularity of 'teamwork' in the business setting gives the illusion of some kind of communal bond, the result of the emphasis on teams, argues Sennett, is actually very different. Temporary, fragile teams put together for short-term tasks and quickly broken up afterwards means a series of short-term, pragmatic relationships. The army of 'facilitators' means that no one takes or learns how to take responsibility for the outcome of such teamwork, opening up more subtle, because unnoticed, forms of power and manipulation in the workplace.

Sennett's point is that all these features of modern flexible work patterns, integral to 'the new capitalism', are destructive of character. They all undermine the features of work and social organization that build traits such as trust, steadfastness, loyalty and commitment. And when character dissolves, it is not surprising that self-esteem, dignity and behaviour do as well.

Sennett has also written more recently on the implications of modern systems of welfare.[7] He develops the concept of 'respect' as a mix of prestige, recognition, honour and dignity, arguing that there is too little of it in contemporary societies.[8] His thesis is that 'modern society lacks positive expressions of respect and recognition to others'. Ours is a society in which dependence is seen as bad thing, independence a desirable quality. But independence does not build community. Nor does it build character, which consists of 'the relational side of personality'.[9] The inequalities of our society, coupled with the meritocracy that dominates social and working relationships, means that it is very hard for those at the bottom of the social scale to earn respect, or even self-respect.

Alain de Botton's *Status Anxiety* looks at similar issues. It examines the different ways in which we establish our place in society and build up a sense of worth through those processes. Contemporary culture is fundamentally meritocratic. Social mobility is a central value of all Western societies, and hence we have a deep belief in self-improvement and the possibility of bettering ourselves socially, financially and emotionally. Whereas pre-modern people tended to accept their place within a strictly ordered hierarchy, now we are less likely to do so, believing instead in the kind of culture of opportunity which makes it possible for us to transcend boundaries of class, geography and origin. De Botton points out that for all its virtues, one of the consequences of this more egalitarian type of society bequeathed to us by the Enlightenment is an increase in the potential for people to envy others: 'The more people we take to be our equals, and compare ourselves to, the more people there will be to envy.'[10] In fact, 'The price we have paid for expecting to be so much more than our ancestors is a perpetual anxiety that we are far from being what we might be.'[11]

A meritocracy has the benefit of allowing greater opportunity and equality for everyone. Yet it has its downsides too. When wealth was simply a sign of fortunate birth, it carried no sense that the rich were ultimately any more valuable or virtuous than those who were poor. In a society where the possession of money is an indicator of hard work, intelligence and ability, it suddenly becomes charged with a new 'moral worth' – it may become a sign that the wealthy really are better, and not just better off, than the poor. In a meritocracy, if you fail to achieve, the system delivers a very harsh judgement: it is because you are not good enough to succeed. In addition, comments de Botton significantly, this change in social values coincided with the time when 'Christianity lost its grip on the imagination of those holding the levers of power and respect for the poor and feelings of community dissipated along with it'.[12]

As a result society is racked with what de Botton calls 'status anxiety', a nervous, troubled worry about one's own true worth, the rampant cancer of envy and jealousy, and chronic self-doubt. These in turn lead to the erosion of some vital building blocks of good social life: trust, mutual concern, self-sacrifice and personal security. As Sennett puts it in the concluding words of *The Corrosion of Character*, 'A regime which provides human beings no deep reasons to care about one another cannot long preserve its legitimacy.'[13]

These two writers point to an element often omitted in discussions between right and left: the notion of character. This is something untouched by financial provision, and it cannot be elicited by social control. It emerges from deeper structural relationships in society, from the stories that we are told and that we tell ourselves about who we are and where we belong. Cries for more police on the street or greater understanding of the causes of poverty both fail to address the issue of the kind of people we are and how personal character might be developed within contemporary societies. Let me give an example.

Building character

Several years ago, I used to help regularly in a local church youth group. Those who attended were white, black or mixed race, most came from disadvantaged backgrounds, and very few were living with both biological parents. One evening I remember one of the regulars in the group – we'll call him Michael – coming into the church hall carrying a pair of car stereo speakers. The conversation went roughly like this:

'Where did you get those, Michael?'
'I found them.'
'Where?'
'Somewhere.'
'Did you nick them?'
'So what if I did?'
'You can't just steal things like that!'

'Why not?'

'Because it's wrong. How would you like it if someone broke into your room and stole your stereo system?'

'I always lock my room.'

"That's not the point.'

'Yes it is. If that stupid p***k had locked his car then he wouldn't have had his speakers nicked. If he's stupid enough to leave it unlocked then he gets what he deserves. It's his own fault. If he leaves the car open, he's asking me to nick it – that's the rules round here.'

The conversation uncovered a gulf in values and a certain skill in logical coherence by this teenage thief. I knew something of Michael's background, was aware that his brother was doing time in prison, that he lived with his mother and several other siblings and was a regular truant from school. Here was someone who lived in a micro-community, made up of his family, friends and some (but not all) of the people who lived on his rundown housing estate, that had its own set of values and norms. The way to win esteem and respect was to show yourself to be adaptable, sharp, on the lookout for a quick and easy way of making money, willing to risk being caught, but always getting away with it. A nonchalant, cool exterior, unfazed by danger, a nimble-footed ability to deceive – all of these were the virtues of his immediate community, fuelled by a story that told them who they were and how they could survive in the world.

The story that controlled Michael's life was clear. He believed that no one else was going to look out for him if he didn't look out for himself. Life was a competition in which, unless he took the slim chances that fortune and other people's carelessness offered him, there was little way out of the relative poverty that had been his experience so far. He also believed he was entitled to whatever he could get his hands on, and that theft was a perfectly valid way of acquiring property. He also believed, rightly so, judging by the looks of admiration from his mates at the time, that such brazen theft was a route to much esteem from his contemporaries. It was his way of earning respect.

Any clever ethical manoeuvres I made to try to outwit him foundered on his self-assured and well-defended moral system of dog-eat-dog, personal improvement at all costs. While disturbed by his nonchalant disregard for others, the encounter did make me wonder what kind of community breeds people like that. He lived, as I did, in a culture that encourages self-improvement, values acquisitiveness and is intensely individualistic. And those three are a dangerous mix. He was enticed, as I was, by the ads that encourage envy, consumption and personal satisfaction. The difference was that I had, through my talents, upbringing and education, a route to achieving the goals of comfort and status. He did not. So he made up, and justified to himself, his own way of getting to where the surrounding culture told him he should be.

Michael's 'rules' might have been different from mine, and from those of the rest of society, but he did not dispute the wider story told by that society – that the way to satisfaction was through the acquisition of goods, which act as a sign of success and prosperity. He also believed that individual rights are sacrosanct and that individuals should aim to lift themselves out of their circumstances to aim for a better life. He just did it in a different way.

He had developed habits of theft and deception through accepting what he had learnt about self-betterment, the acquisition of property and the primacy of the individual. The fact that this particular means of acquiring property violated the rights of another person and broke the 'rules' didn't matter. The only rules he was willing to live by were his own: theft was a means to an end prescribed by the culture in which he lived.

The story illustrates a number of key points. First, character is conditioned by communities. The virtues we strive for tend to be the ones that win us esteem and value in the eyes of our peers. Sporty people will value the discipline required for physical fitness, musicians will esteem the skill required to interpret notes on a page with sensitivity and passion, barristers will value the analytical ability to get to the heart of an argument quickly and the verbal dexterity needed to persuade a jury. A society which values individual achievement, material acquisition and competition will tend to admire people who win. The point is that, despite our protestations about individual autonomy, the kind of community we belong to has a huge say in the kind of people we become.

Second, it shows that it is possible to strive for the goals accepted by society, but through questionable means, as Michael had done. Yet bringing the question of 'character' into play begins to erode that distinction. Prizing 'character' suggests that the kind of people we are might actually be more important than what we might achieve. It is possible to conceive of a community where the main thing to be aimed at was a character marked by such virtues as honesty, kindness, generosity, patience and goodness. Whatever that brought you in terms of career success or material prosperity would be secondary and less important. Esteem and respect would be won by those who had developed those qualities of life, not necessarily by those who had achieved celebrity, wealth or power. It would be a society that did not disdain wealth and meritocratic success, but they would be incidental, of lesser interest to the acquisition of virtue and character. It would be a society in which Michael would actually earn dislike and disdain for acting in the way he did, regardless of how good he was at it.

The question is whether our societies, configured as they are, are capable of producing character or virtue in this sense. Unfortunately, there are strong arguments to say that they cannot.

Liberal societies and the development of character

One of the central features of modern Western societies is their plural nature. Our communities are made up of a wide variety of people of different racial origins, religious traditions, political viewpoints and value systems. It is a short step, however, from the 'fact of plurality' to the 'ideology of pluralism'.[14] While 'plurality' draws attention to the indisputable fact that different people live alongside one another in a cultural mix unknown a century ago, 'pluralism' is the doctrine that suggests that all views are equally valid and true. With this as a basis, we then also need to distinguish between 'cultural pluralism', which claims that while all cultures have their good and bad points, no one culture is better in itself than any other, 'social pluralism', which asserts that it is vital to regulate society so that all viewpoints can coexist peacefully alongside one another, and 'religious pluralism', which maintains that all religious claims are relative and no one religion can claim to be any more true than any other.

It is the second of these, 'social pluralism', that needs attention at this point. Liberal, open, democratic societies effectively adopt a set of rules to regulate relations between different communities. At the macro level they are officially neutral. Political and social liberalism, at its most basic level, is therefore simply a system that arbitrates and sets the ground rules for encounter between different people, groups and perspectives within a plural society. It deliberately does not take sides and has to keep an open public square, with tolerance as the primary virtue.

Can such a society inculcate character and virtue? Liberal societies by definition do not have a common story, a common set of assumptions, beyond the need for broad-mindedness. Such societies could only perceive the inculcation of virtue as an invasion of private space, as there could be no real agreement on which virtues were to be cultivated and in which form. For example, is patience a desirable virtue at all times? In a business setting, excessive patience with an employee who is not producing the goods might be a bad management choice – better to move him on and bring someone in who can do the job as quickly as possible. Is courage in battle for one's country a virtue to be encouraged, when many are not convinced that they should die for something as arbitrary as a nation state, especially if that state is fighting an unjust war? Muslims will hold as a primary virtue submission to the will of Allah; Christians will prize an endless willingness to forgive, seventy times seven and more; secular humanists will value tolerance above all else. As we have seen, virtues depend on stories and communities that are coherent and cohesive. Liberal societies by their very nature encourage coexistence, not coherence. Such societies cannot have their cake and eat it. A society that values competition, individual rights, social improvement and conspicuous consumption cannot at the same time easily maintain community, mutuality and virtue for its own sake. The American Lutheran theologian Gilbert Meilaender puts the dilemma nicely:

> Successful moral education requires a community which does not hesitate to inculcate virtue in the young, which does not settle for the discordant opinions of alternative visions of the good, which worries about what the stories of its poets teach. In short, there can be little serious moral education in a community which seeks only to be what we have come to call 'liberal'.[15]

All this is not, of course, to say that liberalism, democracy and openness in society are bad. Naturally in plural societies, we need to find ways of living together that do not end up in violence or strife. We have to get on. It is simply to point out that, while our culture is reasonably good at that task, it is not good at cultivating virtue. How can it be when there is little moral consensus about what is truly virtuous?

Cultivating virtue

How then is virtue cultivated? Meilaender's solution is to embrace a form of sectarianism. Rather than the liberal agenda of eliding differences between faiths, suppressing the expression of individual beliefs, we should encourage each separate community to do its own job as well as it can in encouraging their own virtues and goodness in their young people, converts and members. Eventually, that process may end up with a new moral vision for the whole of society:

> Each should help his children and friends strive for virtue
> as we fashion our smaller communities of belief and seek to
> transmit the vision which inspires us . . . And perhaps out
> of such sectarianism will arise some smaller communities
> whose vision is so powerful and persuasive that new moral
> consensus will be achieved among us.[16]

Perhaps that is the main challenge for the church today: can it become a community capable of holding its identity and vision so clearly, and teaching it so effectively to its members, that true Christian virtue results? Can it become a community that builds genuine character, enough to forge a new moral vision for the Western world as the church did when the great edifice of Greco-Roman culture fell apart on the eve of the Dark Ages in the sixth century?[17]

Alasdair MacIntyre's book *After Virtue* ended with a call for a new St Benedict – the monk who founded Western monasticism on the eve of the Dark Ages. In other words, in the confusion of contemporary culture, what is needed is a new vision of a way of life that develops the kind of virtue that will build community, not undermine it. Will the contemporary church be capable of forming new communities in which learning, holiness and goodness can be learnt? That is the task to which the church needs to attend with all its strength, not just for the sake of its own survival, but for the sake of our whole society. Brian Appleyard, the British journalist, writes of his hopes for the future:

> Perhaps the least interesting thing about the future is the
> type of technology we shall be using. The most interesting
> thing is what kind of people we shall be. If we can focus on
> this, rather than the gadgets, then we might come up with
> some hopeful, or at least illuminating answers.

What kind of people we shall be? That is the vital question. Our society is desperate to find ways of developing character, integrity and virtue. As our power to create and destroy each other and the planet we live on grows stronger every year, as tensions between rival versions of how life should be lived heighten, the question of how we use such power and how we relate to each other is crucial. Can we develop the qualities that enable us to use our powers responsibly and build communities? The future may depend on it.

The question is also urgent at a more personal level. People who are unable to forgive when they are slighted face a future of bitterness, anger and frustration. Whether the offence is real or imaginary, an inability to forgive harms the one who has been offended more than the offender. It is a vital skill for life. Similarly, people who lack patience will constantly find themselves flying into uncontrollable rages which break friendships and bring on stress. An inability to trust makes few friends and makes long-term relationships impossible. People who are full of themselves, dripping with arrogance and with hardly a trace of humility, are likely to end up with fewer and fewer friends and family who can bear to be with them. Christian virtue has love for others as its central pillar, and so it is uniquely suited to enabling people to develop good healthy relationships in community. It is not rocket science to work out that all of these basic Christian virtues are vital skills for life. We need to learn how to practise them if we are to survive and live well.

Where can you go to learn such things? There is no requirement for courses on Patience in the national curriculum. You cannot get degrees in Kindness from reputable universities. I have never seen further education colleges offering classes in Generosity or Faithfulness. If churches were to become places where ordinary people knew they could go to learn some of the basic skills they need to negotiate life well, think what a difference that might make. What if the local church became known as somewhere ordinary people could go to learn such skills? And what if such people began to learn these qualities in such volume that it began to impact our ways of relating to each other in all kinds of interpersonal relations, changing the social fabric itself?

Would that be to turn the church into a self-help programme, however, diverting its attention away from the central task of preaching the gospel? The short answer is the opposite: it would *return* it to its central task. But that statement needs some backing up, and that is what the next few chapters are designed to provide.

Notes

1   Allan Bloom, *The Closing of the American Mind* (New York: Simon & Schuster, 1987), p. 25.
2   Immanuel Kant, *Grounding for the Metaphysics of Morals*, trans. James W. Ellington, 3rd ed. (Indianapolis: Hackett, 1993), p. 30.
3   *Ibid.*, pp. 44–5.
4   *Ibid.*, p. 38.
5   Richard Sennett, *The Corrosion of Character: The Personal Consequences of Work in the New Capitalism* (New York: Norton, 1998).
6   *Ibid.*, p. 22. Charles Handy describes a similar development in modern working habits as a 'portfolio world', see Charles Handy, *The Empty Raincoat: Making Sense of the Future* (London: Arrow, 1995).
7   Richard Sennett, *Respect: The Formation of Character in an Age of Inequality* (London: Penguin, 2004).
8   *Ibid.*, pp. 53–8.
9   *Ibid.*, p. 53.
10   Alain de Botton, *Status Anxiety* (London: Hamish Hamilton, 2004), p. 47.
11   *Ibid.*, p. 63.
12   *Ibid.*, p. 106.
13   Sennett, *Corrosion of Character*, p. 148.
14   These designations come from Lesslie Newbigin, *The Gospel in a Pluralist Society* (London: SPCK, 1989), p. 14.
15   Gilbert Meilaender, *The Theory and Practice of Virtue* (Notre Dame: University of Notre Dame, 1984), p. 72.
16   *Ibid.*, p. 98.
17   Andrew Walker makes a similar point: 'If . . . the world staggers onwards with more consumption, wrapped up in mass culture, yet splitting at the seams, we will still need to create sectarian plausibility structures in order for our story to take hold of our congregations, and root them in the gospel handed down by our forebears.' Andrew Walker, *Telling the Story: Gospel, Mission and Culture, Gospel and Culture* (London: SPCK, 1996), p. 190.

Chapter 5

Becoming like God

If we were asked what it means to be a Christian, perhaps few of us would come up with the definition tucked away in the back pages of the Bible. We might suggest it consists of knowing God, having our sins forgiven, following Jesus or even going to church. Not many would go so far as to say, as the author of 2 Peter does, that it is to 'participate in the divine nature' (2 Pet. 1.4).

It is a bold claim. It even sounds a little blasphemous, especially in Western Christian ears (Eastern Orthodox Christians would have fewer problems with it). It just seems a bit too presumptuous to suggest that it is God's purpose that we 'participate in the divine nature', or, to put it differently, that we are to become like God. We might be able to cope with the idea of becoming a bit nicer, more pleasant, less angry or resentful, but 'becoming like God' is surely going too far.

There is an old joke that runs: 'Question: what is the difference between God and a lawyer? Answer: God doesn't think he's a lawyer.' The joke reflects our hesitations about wanting to be like God. Surely we are meant to know our place and not aspire to anything as grand as that?

Yet a brief glance into the thought of some of the great theologians of the church should convince us otherwise. Early theologians such as Irenaeus of Lyons, Hilary of Poitiers and Gregory of Nyssa had a word for salvation. That word was *theosis*, which can be translated as 'being made divine'. And if that sounds a bit too Greek and alien, try John Calvin: 'The purpose of the gospel is to render us conformable to God, and, if we may so speak, to deify us.'

Now of course this doesn't mean that we get absorbed into the divine being – that is Hinduism, not Christianity. We retain our humanity and our individuality. We are invited to participate in, not be swallowed up by, divinity. However, the idea remains that while we retain our full humanity, we are still meant to share God's very being. This is not just having 'a relationship with God'. It goes much further than that, to the belief that we can share his very nature. The goal of Christian life is nothing short of this. There can hardly be a greater and more invigorating invitation. It offers and promises a path to personal transformation with a goal much more ambitious and inspiring than physical fitness or inner spiritual serenity.

So what can all this mean? To begin to find an answer to that, we need to take a brief look at the story that informs and shapes Christian character.

The story of the Bible

The book of Genesis is primarily a story that tells us who God is, who we are and what the world is. Its primary aim is not to teach us details of how all these things came about: its main function is theological, not scientific or historical. That, however, does not make it any less true.

In the world of the Bible, nature is not a part of God, an extension of his being and so worshipped as divine, as most Ancient Near Eastern religions suggested. Instead, it exists independently of God, simply because God chose to create something different from himself. Nature is not God and while we are to respect it, we are certainly not to worship it.

Creating space
In his act of creation, out of something 'formless and void', God made a good, wonderful and fertile world. The story gives the sense of God pushing apart constricting forces, separating 'the water under the expanse from the water above it' (Gen. 1.7), creating a space for good things to flourish and grow. And in that space they do. Animal, plant and human life begins to burst out. There is a surging, fertile power about the world as the author

depicts it, like one of those speeded-up films of a garden being planted and coming to life, green shoots, stalks and then flowers appearing in a riot of colour and uncontrolled exuberance. Yet all this energy needs order. Creation is not only an act of letting go and giving space, it is also an act of shaping, like a skilful gardener harnessing the natural growth to bring something beautiful and proportioned out of what might otherwise be chaotic. The process of creation is also described as God shaping, moulding and bringing life and beauty from that empty darkness. Yet this world always exists against a background of nothingness, the chaos that always threatens to undo what God has made and return it to the darkness from which it came. The author of Genesis doesn't try to explain the nature or origin of chaos, he just assumes it. And he presents God as the one who brings order out of disorder, something out of nothing.

Then, out of all creation, he chooses one special part of it to take care of the rest, to bring about and sustain the order it needs if it is to reach its potential and not become wild and destructive. That role is given to humanity. Humans stand with their feet on the earth, not in the heavens. They are in one sense just another part of creation, tied closely to the plants and animals, not standing apart from them at a privileged distance. Yet humanity, out of all the species on the planet, is given a special calling – to 'rule over' the world (Gen. 1.28). This language has of course been controversial in recent times, as the Judaeo-Christian account of the relationship between humanity and the planet has been blamed for environmental disaster. The idea of humans being given dominion over creation conjures up images of a *carte blanche* to abuse, exploit and do as we like with it, leading to polluted rivers, acid rain and global warming. Yet it is perfectly clear from the context that 'rule' involves responsibility. Humanity has been called to care for creation in God's name. It is not a licence for unfettered domination. In fact, it is exactly the opposite. We have been given the responsibility to care for creation in exactly the way God himself would do it. For this purpose God imprints his image upon us – his likeness, so that we are capable of acting in his name in caring for and bringing shape to the created order (Gen. 1.27).[1]

Falling from grace

At this early point of the story, tragedy strikes. Humans decide they are unwilling to play this role. They are not content to rule in God's name, to play their important but limited role in the world, instead wanting to transgress the bounds set for them and rule in their own name. Environmental abuse is not the result of God's calling to humanity – it is the direct outcome of disobedience to that calling.

As a result, the delicate relationships between the different parts of the order of the universe, between God and humanity, and between humanity and the animate and inanimate creation, are fractured. Nature no longer cooperates with humanity, as a flood almost wipes out the known world (Gen. 5–9). Water, originally given to make the earth fertile and to sustain life (Gen. 2.10), now becomes a mortal enemy, threatening to extinguish life from the surface of the planet. Far into the Old Testament mindset, the sea remained a symbol of chaos, the dark forces from which the world was made, threatening to return the world to the emptiness from which it was born.[2] Relations between humans are broken as Adam and Eve blame each other for the fault, and Cain murders his brother Abel. The two closest relations we know – between male and female and between siblings – are both deeply damaged. Relations between humanity and the non-human creation are also broken. Enmity and competition now replace cooperation between animals and humans (3.14–15), and the earth no longer gladly yields its fruit. Instead it becomes hard, reluctant, defiant, and work is no longer a delight but falls under a curse (3.17–19).

The deepest effect, however, is upon humanity itself. The almost naïve, innocent relationships symbolized by nakedness, with nothing to hide from God or anyone else, are replaced by shame, as the man and the woman hide from God (3.8). When you find yourself hiding from a former friend as he approaches, it's a sure sign that the relationship has gone sour. God has to make them coverings to hide their shame from each other (2.25; 3.21). Humanity, this special part of creation chosen to bear the image of God, to look like him, act like him and reflect his character, now finds that image, though not entirely extinguished, shattered and defaced. It is important to grasp what this means, as it is crucial for the story we are telling.

A picture might convey the point. Imagine angels visiting the earth, expecting to find humanity made in the image of God, resembling him and playing their part in the created order in his name, as they were always meant to do. Taking one look at us, they mutter to each other, 'They don't look much like God any more.' That is what it means when we say that the image of God in humanity is broken. It means we are no longer good, reliable reminders of God and his providential care for his world. We no longer reflect his nature as we were intended to do. We no longer look or act much like him.

In consequence, God sets limits on human powers. The man and the woman are banished from the garden of delight (which is the meaning of 'Eden'), in case they grasp the ultimate power that they would now inevitably abuse (3.22). He breaks up their common language, to stop them conspiring to dominate the earth and replace God (Gen. 11). Yet at the same time he also sets limits on the very evil they have unleashed. Cain may have killed his brother Abel, yet God still places a mark on him so that his life is preserved despite his crime (4.15).

In the middle of chapter 11 of the book of Genesis, the story is at its lowest point. If this were a film, it would require sombre music against a desolate, bleak landscape, as the hope with which the story began just a few chapters earlier has all but vanished. Yet almost immediately, a small shaft of light breaks through as the scene shifts to a family growing unnoticed somewhere in the desert lands of the Middle East.

A frail hope

Out of this disaster one man, Abraham, is called to be the means through which God wishes to bless this damaged world. He and his family are meant to be the bearers and embodiment of the message that God has not given up on his world. The story told through the Old Testament continues as a search for a man 'after God's own heart', someone to whom God can entrust power. A succession of characters are led centre stage, yet none of them quite fits the bill. Abraham's own family proves dysfunctional. Sarah's childlessness leads to his weak-willed complicity in the plan to short-circuit God's intentions by siring a child through a slave woman. Sarah laughs at God rather than trusting his promise. Abraham even tries to deceive a powerful king by passing off Sarah as his sister. It is hard to escape the conclusion that Abraham, though occasionally full of stubborn courage, is characterized by deception, cowardice and weakness. Isaac also plays the 'my-wife-is-really-my-sister' trick (Gen. 26), Jacob cheats his brother out of his birthright, Moses commits murder and allows Aaron to lead the people into idolatry, and yet God remains grimly faithful to this family, guiding them into a land of their own.

The judges who lead the people in their early years in the Promised Land prove to be no better than the patriarchs, displaying vanity, recklessness and arrogance in equal measure. This is hardly a moral tale, offering us examples to follow. It is instead an ambivalent catalogue of morally feeble people stumbling along by grace rather than natural wit or goodness. Eventually the people cry out for a king, and despite the misgivings of Samuel (1 Sam. 8), and in the later tradition, of prophets like Hosea, offering various versions of 'I told you so' (e.g. Hos. 8.4), they get one. The first, Saul, is no better than anyone else. Yet the one who follows comes closer to the ideal than anyone. Although still deeply flawed,[3] there is something about David that makes him a 'man after God's own heart' (1 Sam. 13.14). It is to David that the promise comes. Despite the miserable failure of the family of Abraham to produce the new Adam, the one who will rule wisely over God's chosen people, God will one day bring a new king from the family of David who will rule in God's name in the way humankind was always meant to. His kingdom will last for ever and he will build a new temple in which God will at last dwell on earth again.

Samuel was right. Despite these promising signs, the monarchy turns out to be a major disappointment. David's sons fall to squabbling over the succession, and before too long the arguments have led to a fatal division of the nation into the northern kingdom (Israel) and the southern kingdom (Judea). The division so weakens the nation that it becomes easy prey to any passing tyrant. Inevitably, the northern kingdom is swallowed up by the Assyrian empire in 722 BC and is lost for ever. In the south, Jerusalem finally falls to the Babylonians in 587 BC. The kings have failed. Exile begins and the hopes of God finding a ruler to wield power in his name, the new Adam, are at their lowest ebb since Babel.

Yet again, just as the calling of Abraham shone a light of hope into the gloom, the note of hope still sounds, even as the exile continues, and the pages of the Old Testament draw to a close. The exilic prophets, despite their doom-laden tone, all have moments of anticipation, often focused around the promise given to David and his line, that God will one day send a true King, the Son of David (Zechariah and Jeremiah), rebuild his temple (Ezekiel and Haggai), give his people a new heart and spirit (Ezekiel), forgive their sins (Micah), defeat their enemies and bring them home (Jeremiah and Amos).

The return of the King

Jesus is born into a nation torn between hope and despair. Hope that the promises are about to be fulfilled is mixed with despair over the state of the people, subject to the tyranny of the Roman empire. As the Gospel writers tell the story of Jesus, all these themes come up again and again. Jesus is the Son of David, the one who embodies the rule or kingdom of God, and who ushers it in. He will rebuild the temple, send a new Spirit into people's hearts, bring forgiveness and restoration, defeat their enemies and bring them home. Yet these promises are fulfilled in ways few expected. The temple is his body, which will be raised after three days. The enemies to be defeated are not the Romans, but the real enemies of humankind: sin, death and hell. The restoration of Israel is not the restoration of their land, but the promise of blessing for the whole of the earth, with the Gentiles now brought into God's people.

Ever since Adam and Eve fell from grace, God had, as it were, been searching for a man after his own heart, someone to whom he could entrust power over creation. He was looking for someone who could do what Adam was meant to do: bring order, harmony and beauty to his world, restraining and defeating the powers of chaos and darkness that threatened to return it from whence it came. Despite some promising candidates, none proved up to the task. Yet somehow the waiting is part of the point, showing the grandeur of the answer when it comes. Now God has finally found what he has been looking for. The fact that Jesus performs miracles is theologically very significant. These are not impressive tricks, performed to convince sceptical cynics to believe in him. They are signs that say that here at last is someone to whom God can entrust power. Jesus walks on lakes and calms storms, subduing water, the symbol of destruction and chaos. He heals the sick and raises the dead. He produces bread from stone and feeds the hungry with meagre resources. He uses his power to do what God himself would do – to rule wisely and justly. It is as if God could not entrust that power to anyone else, as they would abuse it. For most of us, power corrupts. For the Son of God, it does not.

It is significant that when Paul comes to discuss the meaning of the arrival of Jesus the Messiah, he repeatedly compares Jesus to Adam (Rom. 5.12–14; 1 Cor. 15.22, 45). Jesus is for him the second Adam, the one who perfectly reflects the image of God (Col. 1.15), the one who does what Adam was intended to do. Jesus Christ is a picture for us of perfect divinity and of perfect humanity at the same time: he does what only God can do, raising the dead, rebuilding the temple and defeating the enemies of mankind, but he does so as a man, fully human in every way.

Christians, followers of Christ, indwelt by his Spirit, are those who are 'in Christ', called to grow into his likeness: 'predestined to be conformed to the likeness of his Son' (Rom. 8.29), and more explicitly still, 'just as we have borne the likeness of the earthly man [i.e. Adam], so shall we bear the likeness of the man from heaven' (1 Cor. 15.49).[4] Just as Christ is the second Adam, bearing the very imprint of God's image, so in Christ that image is to be restored to the rest of humanity. Because the forgiveness of sins, the resurrection and the gift of the Spirit are all now freely available in Christ, those who become followers of Christ are meant to be 'transformed into his likeness with ever-increasing glory, which comes from the Lord, who is the Spirit' (2 Cor. 3.18). They are to become spiritually healthy.

The purpose of the gospel, then, is not just to save a few people for heaven. It is to create a new kind of person, ready to dwell in the new heavens and the new earth that are being prepared. The promise given in the New Testament is not that we are to be whisked away into some ghostly paradise, leaving this world behind. It is ultimately the promise of a renewed and transformed earth (2 Pet. 3.13; Rev. 21.1), indwelt by new people with new bodies, with the image of God restored in them through Christ and the Spirit, dwelling in it.[5] As C. S. Lewis once put it, 'God became man to turn creatures into sons: not simply to produce better men of the old kind, but to produce a new kind of man.'[6]

This means that transformation, holiness, discipleship, sanctification, spiritual fitness, or whatever you want to call it, is not an optional extra for those who take Christianity a bit more seriously than others. It is the point of the whole exercise. God forgives and rescues sinners precisely so that he can turn them into people who resemble Christ and share in his image, participating in the divine nature. His purpose is to transform us into people who are capable of fulfilling the calling he gave us at the start: to rule over creation in his name. That involves using power not for our own ends or glory, but in God's name, so that the new heaven and new earth might be peopled with those who will not (as Adam did) take the power given to them and abuse it, but will learn to rule as God does – with gentleness and justice.

Just as the fitness industry has a very clear idea of the kind of bodies we are supposed to have – an ideal to strive for – Christians have, or should have, a very clear idea of spiritual perfection, spiritual fitness. To be spiritually fit is to be like Jesus. It means to become more fully human. It means to become like God.

Becoming like God

What does that mean? Occasionally, when ethical issues such as the legalization of euthanasia or capital punishment are debated, we make the point that doctors or judges must not 'play God'. The implication is that to be like God means to be immensely powerful, to have ultimate sway over the fate of other people, to do as we wish with them. Alternatively, when we say of someone, 'She thinks she's God', it is not the most complimentary thing we could say about a person. On other occasions, we might say of an Adonis-type person with a finely toned body, bronzed and muscular, that they are 'like a god'. Or we look at supremely talented individuals – sportspeople like Muhammad Ali or Michael Jordan, or musicians like Elvis Presley or Madonna – and treat them as gods. There has been a famous piece of graffiti on a wall by the side of the main road from Oxford to London for about 40 years now, which simply declares, 'Clapton is God.' In the UK, Nigella Lawson has made a decent living out of teaching women how to be 'domestic goddesses', those whose soufflés always rise, whose clothes and house decor are at the cutting edge of fashion, whose children always behave impeccably, whose demeanour is eternally calm and serene, despite combining a successful career with 'divine' cooking and wise parenting. Do these pictures really reflect what it means to be 'like God'?

They may reflect various versions of the gods (for example the Adonis image of the athlete reflects some ancient Greek ideas of what a god looked like), but they do not describe the Christian God.

The God of the biblical story displays very different characteristics from the Greek gods, or even the gods of Eastern faiths. He is not capricious but faithful, keeping his promises and covenants from generation to generation. He is not a sea of placid detachment from the world, but instead interacts with it. He gets angry, though not unpredictably or wildly. His anger is reserved for those who abuse his precious creation, especially the people within it. He is not some fiery Zeus, standing on Olympus terrifying and demanding attention. Instead he is humble, lavishly creating a world in which he remains hidden, a world that is not full of signs demanding we pay him attention and give him his due. The qualities that mark him out are those of patience, faithfulness, perseverance, kindness, goodness, self-control, humility, joy, creativity and, above all, love.

In short, the God of the Bible is just like Jesus. His path leads not to spiritual enlightenment and inner peace, but to a bloody and excruciatingly painful death. This contrast points up starkly the difference between Christian understandings of the 'perfect soul' and the ones we find in the 'mind, body, spirit' world of today. Of course this could be taken as a Christian glorification of suffering, a kind of spiritual masochism. Yet the cross has a clear meaning and purpose in Christian theology. It is a demonstration of divine love. As John puts it, 'This is how we know what love is: Jesus Christ laid down his life for us' (1 Jn 3.16).

In other words, and as simply as we can possibly put it, a Christian understanding of spiritual health is that it involves a capacity to love until it hurts. Inner tranquillity and peace are present in the New Testament picture of the perfect soul, but they are not centre stage. The goal is quite different. Someone who through yoga or reiki (or even Christianity) experienced inner serenity and harmony, yet shunned the hard details of giving and offering painful, long-term persevering love to ageing parents, difficult children or irritating neighbours would in New Testament terms be an unhealthy human being. The person who possesses the 'perfect soul' is instead the one who, however plagued by doubts and inner struggles, still displays a capacity to go on loving her friends, and even at the utmost her rivals and opponents.

For humans to reflect the divine nature means to share exactly the qualities of God, which we see to perfection in Jesus Christ. That is how the angels would recognize God in us again, if we displayed these particular virtues. We do not become God-like through the kind of things we normally aspire to, such as wealth, sexual attractiveness, talent or success. We have seen in our own culture what happens when those become the centre of aspiration. We become God-like when we learn the virtues of love, joy, peace, patience, kindness, goodness, faithfulness, gentleness and self-control (Gal. 5.22–23).

These qualities are not only divine qualities, they also happen to be the ones that will make us truly happy, productive and fruitful. Fundamental to this kind of thinking is the conviction that, however good physical pleasures are, 'goodness and wisdom make us happier than food and sex'.[7] That is a secret that very few people know today, partly because sex and gluttony are everywhere recommended, but also because our societies do not know how to cultivate goodness and wisdom. So we strain after food, sex and money, good things, to be sure, but they can never make us ultimately happy on their own. Meanwhile we ignore goodness and wisdom, which alone can. There is a deep synergy between the character of the God revealed in the Scriptures and the qualities we need to live good and contented lives. This is a God of faithfulness, hope and love – he keeps his promises, gives hope and showers his creation with love. So it is no surprise that in relationship with a God like this, we might expect to learn how to trust, how to hope and how to love.

These are also the characteristics that enable societies to function properly. God's purpose is to produce people who are capable of handling power wisely and for the benefit of the weak, not themselves – people whose use of power is shaped by love, trust and hope. Such people will run businesses with integrity and a regard for people before profits. They will wield political authority with wisdom and justice, rather than as a means of gaining personal status or power. They will be capable of being wise and selfless parents, generous employers and conscientious citizens. They will not take bribes, or be susceptible to illicit favours. They will give generously and redistribute wealth without being forced to. They will care for the poor, and think of creative ways to build self-respect and restore dignity. In a consumer society of endless choice they will make wise and healthy choices, not selfish and destructive ones. As we have already seen, these are features created not so much by laws as by persons. Respect and dignity come through being treated that way in actual personal relations. These people will display the kind of character that legislation cannot produce nor a liberal society cultivate. They will confront evil and injustice with courage and perseverance. They will not always be popular or universally praised, but at the same time these are the kind of people whom you can trust.

Remember who you are

This chapter has outlined the biblical story that tells us who God is, what this world is, where it came from and where it is going. It also tells us who we humans are. The problem for most of us is that we forget who we are and settle for something less than the best.

The Disney film *The Lion King* is the story of a young lion cub, born to the ruler of the animal kingdom. He witnesses his father's death, thinking (wrongly) that he had caused it. Skulking away into the depths of the jungle, he spends his time with a couple of wasters, a likeable meercat and a warthog. As he grows, he becomes comfortable with his surroundings and yet something nags away at his soul. One night he has a vision of his father in the evening clouds, speaking to him. The apparition says two very simple things to him: 'Remember who you are. You are more than what you have become.'

It is hard to think of a more appropriate message to twenty-first-century people: 'Remember who you are. You are more than what you have become.' We are creations of the most high God, who made us to take care of the rest of creation on his behalf. We have dignity and worth, not because of our own personal characteristics, but because God has made us and called us, uniquely out of all creation, to bear his image and reflect his glory. We are called to be like God. And we settle for just being nice.

The use and abuse of power

The first few chapters of this book tried to put our discussion into context, a context where the church is failing to provide an attractive product within a consumer society. Yet that society is suffering a crisis of character, longing for personal and individual well-being, yet torn between that and the need for common values in society. More seriously, due to its plural nature, it is unable to create long-term settled character or virtue.

Yet the cultivation of such virtue is vital. The story we have just told, the story of the search for someone capable of wielding power over the world, has a very contemporary ring to it.

The powers that lie in our grasp today are frightening – power to destroy life through arms, to control life through genetics, to waste the planet through environmental abuse. As competing and apparently irreconcilable visions of life jostle ever more closely together in the increasingly crowded global village, the potential for cataclysm through the 'clash of civilizations' grows ever greater. We have learnt to master nature. We have also discovered the power to destroy it.

The revolt against authority has come about in large measure because that authority has been abused so badly. Figures who used to be unquestioned repositories of wisdom and authority are routinely distrusted. The reasons are not hard to find. Examples are numerous of leaders abusing their power: parents who neglect, teachers who victimize, doctors who kill, politicians who lie, clergy who abuse. As a result, one of the common features of postmodern culture is a deep suspicion of power. Claims to truth are in reality veiled attempts to exercise control. According to Michel Foucault, it is power that produces truth, not the other way round. Theorists like Foucault want to make us suspicious of anyone who tries to tell us the truth: 'My point is not that everything is bad, but that everything is dangerous.'[8]

The difficulty is that you can't build a society on suspicion. If you do, it quickly seizes up. Of course accountability is vital, but ultimately, if no one trusts anyone in authority, the resulting checks, balances, reviews, investigations and enquiries clog up the system so that nothing gets done. It also breeds a community that is not particularly pleasant to live in. So we are faced with another dilemma. We would like to trust those in authority over us, but we are not sure that we can. And the more we find out about them, the less we do.

Who are the people we can entrust with power, who will use it for the sake of the powerless and not abuse it for their own purposes? Those who have developed the very qualities of God, the qualities that make us fully human: patience, faithfulness, perseverance, kindness, goodness, self-control, humility, joy, creativity and, above all, love. These people will use power wisely and will not be distorted by it. The Bible tells the story of how people are to be restored in the image of God, and how these qualities are to be cultivated in them. It addresses the most urgent question of our times – the need to develop people who not only display 'well-being', but who, through a process of steady, purposeful transformation, are capable of goodness and virtue.

Notes

1   The scene where God brings all the 'beasts of the field and the birds of the air' to be named by the man and woman (Gen. 2.19–20) symbolizes humanity's calling to bring order to the world by the gift of language. Taxonomy is a truly human calling!

2   For example, the sea is the home of monsters such as the Leviathan (Job 3.8; Ps. 74.14, Isa. 27.1), the exodus is the great act of deliverance of Israel from the waters that threatened to cover them as they escaped from Egypt. It is significant that in the book of Revelation, a sign of the coming kingdom is that the sea is banished (Rev. 21.1: 'Then I saw a new heaven and a new earth, for the first heaven and the first earth had passed away, and there was no longer any sea').

3   While a great hero of Israel, David is also a liar, cheat, adulterer and murderer, and that is only with reference to his arranging of Uriah's murder and the theft of his wife Bathsheba, to say nothing of his later indulgence of his sons and weak leadership.

4   See also 2 Cor. 3.18: 'And we, who with unveiled faces all reflect the Lord's glory, are being transformed into his likeness with ever-increasing glory, which comes from the Lord, who is the Spirit.'

5   See N. T. Wright, *What St Paul Really Said: Was Paul of Tarsus the Real Founder of Christianity?* (Oxford: Lion, 1997), ch. 8, 'God's Renewed Humanity', for an excellent short exposition of this point.

6   C. S. Lewis, *Mere Christianity* (London: Geoffrey Bles, 1952), p. 178. Lewis's famous book is in fact another excellent exposition of exactly the kind of theological story I have been developing here, but in a different mode.

7   Ellen Charry, *By the Renewing of Your Minds: The Pastoral Function of Christian Doctrine* (New York: OUP, 1997), p. 132.

8   Paul Rabinow, ed., *The Foucault Reader: An Introduction to Foucault's Thought* (London: Penguin, 1984), p. 343.

Chapter 6

Faith and virtue

At this point, a number of objections might well be rearing their heads. Is that really the message of the Bible? Is all this talk about virtue really just another way of recommending justification by works? Doesn't it all sound a bit too much like hard work?

Ever since the Reformation, Protestants have believed that salvation consists of receiving the forgiveness of sins. This is a gift accepted by faith, not achieved by human virtue. They have also tended to think of conversion as an instant change, of justification as something received by faith in a moment of decision, not a lifetime of moral effort. The idea of growing in virtue might encourage Christians to begin trusting in their works and moral success, and not in Christ.

Karl Barth was perhaps the twentieth century's most influential Protestant theologian. For him, 'the fundamental image for the Christian life is not growth but repetition'.[1] What is needed, according to Barth, is not growth in virtue, but repetition of the Word of God. Christian acts are simply repeated responses to God's word of grace, not evidence of growth in character. For Barth, God's work for our sanctification comes 'new every morning'. Each day we are accepted by grace as the sinners we are, with no sense that we make progress in behaviour, are on a journey towards a goal, or grow into the divine image:

> All attempts . . . to impart to our action anything in the nature of a divine likeness, signify at once and automatically apostasy from Jesus Christ, the denial of the divine grace by which we live, and therefore a relapse into disobedience.[2]

Strong stuff. But it speaks vividly of Barth's belief that if virtue becomes any kind of automatic reaction rather than a conscious response to God's grace, we lose our basic trust in God – and if we lose our trust in God, we lose our salvation. If we did begin to think that we are gradually shaped into the image of God in Christ, then Barth's fear is that it would lead us into independence from God and his grace, as though we no longer needed it for our day-to-day living.

What are we to make of these fears? Do they mean we should avoid speaking of virtue as tainted by association or as a dangerous path to self-sufficiency? One way of approaching this is to take a close look at the central figure in the drama of the Reformation, a figure who above all others seemed to insist that life was not about the cultivation of a virtuous self but about faith in God's promise of grace: Martin Luther.

Luther and virtue

The two most influential figures in Western intellectual history who have written on the virtues are the fourth-century BC philosopher Aristotle, and the thirteenth-century theologian, Thomas Aquinas. Aristotle's thought was used as a structure for developing a new way of presenting and systematizing Christian theology in the Middle Ages. This system became known as scholasticism, a term which referred not so much to the content of theological ideas as to the systematic way they were explored and described. Aquinas was perhaps the greatest exponent of scholastic theology, and his approach is a blend of the Bible, the early Fathers of the church and Aristotle. There is a clear historical and intellectual link between these two figures, and they were both firmly in Luther's firing line as the Reformation began.

We have already noticed Aristotle's fondness for an ethics of virtue. Luther roundly blamed that for many of the ills of the late medieval Catholic Church. Aristotle's *Nicomachean Ethics* basically teaches that we become good by doing good things. If we practise certain actions long and hard enough, then they become habitual and we genuinely become good people. Luther felt that this advice was disastrous. It led Christians to believe that the key to salvation was doing good works, regularly and often. It had in the past led him to believe that too, and the results were catastrophic. It drew him into the depths of uncertainty and doubt. Had he done enough of these good acts? Was he really good all the way through, or was his heart still far from God? If the key to salvation was the acquisition of virtue, then that could only be bad news for someone like Luther, who was sensitive and wise enough to know his own selfishness, pride and avarice. Aristotle also encouraged a kind of morality that affected outward behaviour but did not address the heart, which after all was the part that God was really interested in.

Luther felt it was all too superficial. He criticized Aristotle mercilessly. Referring to the theologians in the University of Paris who had swallowed Aristotle hook, line and sinker, he wrote:

> . . . it is the Parisian school that is condemned in this connection, that impure and foul whore which has declared that Aristotle's teachings on morals are not in conflict with the teachings of Christ, since he teaches nothing other than that virtue is acquired by works, saying, 'By doing good we become good.' The Christian conscience curses this statement as bilge water of hell and says, 'By believing in a Christ who is good, I, even I, am made good: his goodness is mine also, for it is a gift from him and is not my work.'[3]

Luther was not much more complimentary about Aquinas. Commenting on his famous girth, he told a dinner party audience a scurrilous anecdote: 'St Thomas had such a large paunch that he could eat a whole goose at one sitting; and in order for him to have room to sit at the table, a hole had to be cut in the table to accommodate his paunch.'[4] The story may or may not be true, but behind the anatomical insult lies a theological one. Sitting at table with his students, Luther uttered his verdict on Aquinas: 'Thomas is not worth a louse; and the same goes for his writings.' He goes further to put his finger explicitly on the relationship between Aristotle and Aquinas, a criticism with a double barb:

> This great man [Aquinas] is to be pitied not only for attempting to draw his opinions in matters of faith from Aristotle, but also for attempting to base them on a man whom he did not understand, thus building an unfortunate superstructure upon an unfortunate foundation.[5]

As a result of the emphasis on human works as the key to salvation, it seemed the whole of medieval Christendom was feverishly running around trying to perform more and more religious works, becoming more and more virtuous, all with the hope that becoming better people would persuade God to look with favour on them. The idea of virtue became bound up with a particular method of attaining it. Luther, on the other hand, came to believe that we are made good not by works but by faith. This statement is more complex than meets the eye, so needs some explanation.

How to be good

Every medieval theologian agreed that goodness, or righteousness (*iustitia*) to give it its more common medieval name, was essential if humans were to be acceptable before God. The question was, how was this goodness achieved? Answers varied among the different theological schools of the time, but generally speaking most people thought that it came about by some kind of cooperation between God and individual men and women. God's grace is available to help us develop qualities of real goodness within ourselves. With a little effort on our part and God's help, we can grow in goodness, acquire merit before God, and when this process is complete, after many years in purgatory once this life is over, we can be accepted into the very presence of God himself, having been perfected.

Luther thought this went about it the wrong way. For him, we were never meant to be justified (brought into a right relationship with God) by our own goodness, with or without God's help. Instead, he came to believe that justification is granted to us not because of a level of goodness or righteousness that we generate within ourselves, but on account of the goodness or righteousness of Jesus Christ. Jesus is the only truly righteous one, and in the act of faith in him we receive his goodness, his righteousness.

An illustration might help at this point. When I was still at school, Britain changed its currency from the old pounds, shillings and pence to the decimal system. After that time, if you wanted to buy a bus ticket, the old currency would be no use. You could offer as many old pounds and shillings as you liked, but it made no difference – it was simply the wrong currency. What you needed was 'new pence' as they were called then. You had to offer the right currency to get what you needed. It is a little like that with Luther's view of 'works'. Religious actions, good works that we do, are simply the wrong currency. We can multiply them as much as we like, but they will not get us where we need to be, because they don't count. The currency that does count is the goodness of Christ. Christ's righteousness is received not by earning it or qualifying for it through a certain level of spiritual devotion or fitness, but simply by trusting God's promise that all those who believe in Christ are made righteous without any prior works or merits of their own.

According to Luther, then, we receive this righteousness, are justified or made good in God's eyes, by faith and not by works. His point is that a relationship with God has to be based on trust, just like any good human relationship. Conditional friendships are not healthy. A friendship where you have to keep on proving yourself over and over again is not a good one. Strong bonds, such as good marriages, are always founded on simple trust that can be relied on, and it is no different with God.

So perhaps we can begin to see why Aristotle's and Aquinas's way of talking about virtue alarmed Luther He thought it directed people to the wrong place, and made them try to hoard and then offer a wrong and outdated currency. It encouraged people to try to establish their own goodness, when what they needed was Christ's. It was pastorally, psychologically and theologically damaging.

Christ's goodness and ours

Luther said, 'By believing in a Christ who is good, I, even I, am made good: his goodness is mine also, for it is a gift from him and is not my work.' Yet this is not some kind of fiction whereby God pretends we are better than we really are. For Luther, it is the precondition for actually becoming good in our actions and behaviour, and not just our status before God. For Luther, medieval theology not only misunderstood the crucial role of the goodness of Christ, it also misunderstood the way in which we really do become good in ourselves.

The starting point was not trying to get a little better, but heading in the opposite direction altogether, realizing how selfish, compromised and indolent we really are, and at the same time trusting in Christ's goodness, not our own, for salvation. From that point, however, God begins the work of really transforming us so that we become in fact and action what we already are in status and in faith.

During an argument with a theologian called Latomus, Luther made an important distinction.[6] Christians are pure, righteous saints because of the goodness of Christ, which is now theirs by faith, despite the existence of sin in their lives. On the other hand, baptism, which for Luther is one of the main forms in which the gospel comes to us, 'does not remove all sins; it indeed removes all, but not their substance. The power of all, and much of the substance are taken away. Day by day the substance is removed so that it may be utterly destroyed.'[7]

'Day by day' – there is the other element in becoming good.

Faith means that God no longer counts our sins against us. Disciplines then remove the continued presence of those sins from us. The remaining substance of sin, the rubbish left behind by it, as it were, is to be removed through a daily process of transformation. Luther goes on to make a distinction between God's *grace*, which justifies him by faith, and his *gift*, which 'heals from sin and from all the corruption of body and soul'. The Christian is 'forgiven through grace, but as yet, not everything is healed through the gift'. Multiplying metaphors, Luther says this 'gift' of God is like yeast that begins to work its way through the dough, making it rise and change, 'to purge away the sin for which a person has already been forgiven, and to drive out the evil guest for whose expulsion permission has been given'.[8]

How do these two fit together? How does Christ's goodness generate ours? For Luther, justification works backwards, or eschatologically, to give it its full theological name. That means that once our faith is in Christ, God is committed to making us good not just in status but also in fact. So God declares in the present the judgement that one day he will announce over us – that we are fully righteous in every sense. God anticipates the final result of his work in us and treats us in the present as we will one day be. A medical analogy helps Luther explain the point:

It is similar to the case of a sick man who believes the doctor who promises him a sure recovery and in the meantime obeys the doctor's order in the hope of the promised recovery and abstains from those things which have been forbidden him, so that he may in no way hinder the promised return to health or increase his sickness until the doctor can fulfil his promise to him. Now is this sick man well? The fact is that he is both sick and well at the same time. He is sick in fact, but he is well because of the sure promise of the doctor, whom he trusts and who has reckoned him as already cured, because he is sure that he will cure him; for he has already begun to cure him and no longer reckons to him a sickness unto death . . . He has begun to heal him, having promised him the most complete cure unto eternal life.[9]

One day we will be cured, made good, as we grow into the likeness of Christ, yet the crucial thing is that God does not wait to see if we get there before he pronounces us good. He does it now. He covers us with the goodness of Christ, like a warm cloak covering a cold, wet traveller, until she is brought home and warmed by the fire so that she becomes warm in herself. One day our bodily and spiritual natures, our outer and inner natures (to use Luther's language), will coincide, but until then we rest under the knowledge that God has already pronounced his verdict on those whose trust is in Christ: they are already regarded by him as good, just as they will one day be so in fact. God is also committed to making us good in ourselves, to transforming us over time so that we do look, act and think like Christ.

As Luther puts it elsewhere, 'to be holy and to be saved are two entirely different things',[10] but grace does both. God forgives, justifies and declares righteous. He also gradually works to remove sin and build virtue. But the two are essentially linked, in that the former is the essential precondition of the latter. The 'works righteousness' from which Luther turned away was wrong because it didn't make people good: all it did was make people anxious about their salvation, pouring all their energies into religious works such as pilgrimages, indulgences and the like, which were of little benefit to anyone, instead of really being free to give themselves and their goods to their neighbour in love.

Free from such anxiety, the process of daily rooting out sin and building Christian character through discipline and spiritual exercise becomes less fraught or heavy, precisely because our salvation does not hang upon it. It becomes 'safe', to use Gilbert Meilaender's word.[11] Our goodness becomes less of a self-centred analytical process of self-help, and more the growth of habits of love and compassion for others, because the need to perform such actions for one's own sake, to become good in a self-conscious way, has gone. It is as if for Luther the virtues depend on Virtue. We must first be good before we can become good, not the other way round. Truly good acts can only be done by truly good people. As Luther puts it: 'Good works do not make a good man, but a good man does good works.'[12] Aristotle had tried to address the problem of doing, whereas the deeper issue was being. For Luther, what we *are* lies deeper than what we *do*. More importantly still, what we are tends to determine what we do, and that was what Aristotle didn't understand.

If we follow Luther's argument, then Karl Barth's fears about growing into the image of God are groundless – as long as we keep this distinction between Christ's righteousness by which we are saved, and our own righteousness which develops out of the first kind, by which we glorify God. But that still leaves a further question: how is virtue encouraged? How does God go about this process of changing us so that we become in reality and action what we already are in hope and faith?

The law in the Christian life

Lutherans and crypto-Lutherans in other denominations have argued over this for some time. In particular, some have been nervous that any sense of virtue or goodness can be achieved through the exercise of spiritual disciplines. After Luther's death, a debate raged among his successors for years over something called the 'third use of the law'. Clearly, following Luther, God's law, which told us what we must and must not do, was not meant as a means of salvation. What then was the point of the law? Theologians came up with two main uses. The first was to reveal sin by showing how far we have fallen short of God's standards. This was usually known as the theological use of the law. The second was to restrain ungodliness in wider society, through the enactment and enforcement of legislation by duly appointed governing authorities. This was usually known as the political use of the law.

Most Protestant theologians agreed with those two, but differed sharply over a proposed third use, the 'didactic use', which claimed that the law was also useful as a guide to right behaviour for true Christians. Theologians who advocated this use of the law included Luther's right-hand man in Wittenberg, Philip Melanchthon, and the Genevan reformer John Calvin, who in fact made this third use of the law its primary function. They believed that the law should be preached to Christians to show them how to behave and live in conformity to God's design. Fearing anarchic, antinomian chaos if there were no place for instruction on right and appropriate behaviour, they saw the biblical law as the divine blueprint for human life and therefore believed it should be duly taught to Christian people. Opponents who disagreed with this, such as Johann Agricola and later Nicolas Amsdorf and Flacius Illyricus, believed that the gospel alone, and not the law, needs to be preached to Christians.[13] Good works are produced automatically as believers hear the message that they are forgiven, justified and cleansed purely by grace. The law has no place in the life of the Christian and to reintroduce it, as Melanchthon and others were doing, was to lead the Protestant churches back into the legalism from which they had just escaped.

Luther had said and written things that could support both sides of this debate. In so far as it was a debate about what Luther really meant, it was hard to resolve. The real debate was between those who were afraid of returning to Catholic legalism, and those who were afraid of a formless, undisciplined laxness in Protestant life and societies which would bring discredit on the whole movement.

Those who remain nervous about this 'third use' will argue that proper Christian behaviour is brought about by repeating the simple gospel message. The message of grace creates its own response of gratitude and goodness, without any need for the stern shadow of the law. They will also be cautious about any idea that we can develop virtue which builds up as a habit over time. Telling Christians what to do seems to compromise the central principle of Christian freedom. We are not under law, but under grace, so that there can be no spiritual demands made on

Christians. Christian behaviour is either an automatic response to God's grace and favour or it is nothing. It explains why many Protestants are more at home with the verse that talks about Christian qualities being 'fruit of the Spirit' (Gal. 5.22 – implying natural, unmanufactured growth) than with the idea of 'working out your own salvation in fear and trembling' (Phil. 2.12 – implying effort and hard work).

Do Protestants do virtue?

Let's take a look back at Luther. He often talks as if Christian behaviour arises spontaneously and naturally, out of thankfulness, joy and delight in God:

> A Christian man who lives in this confidence towards God knows all things, can do all things, ventures everything that needs to be done, and does everything gladly and willingly, not that he may gather merits and good works, but because it is a pleasure for him to please God in doing these things. He simply serves God with no thought of reward, content that his service please God.[14]

Does that mean that the Christian has to do nothing, trusting that his life will change automatically, without any effort on his part?

The Freedom of a Christian, a short treatise addressed to Pope Leo X on the eve of Luther's excommunication in 1520, was perhaps one of the finest pieces he ever wrote, a work which he claimed contains 'the whole of Christian life in a brief form'.[15] The early part of the essay contains a vital distinction: 'Man has a twofold nature, a spiritual and a bodily one,' In the first part he writes of the 'spiritual' nature, about the meaning and benefits of faith along the lines we have already explained. Faith alone brings righteousness and freedom to the 'inner man'. Later he turns to the other part of his distinction, the 'outer man'.

To those who argue that faith is all that is needed for the

Christian and actions are unnecessary, he replies that this is to misunderstand the nature of human beings. We are not just inner, spiritual people, but we also have an outer, physical, bodily nature, which needs to be brought into conformity to the spirit. Here discipline, order and progress are needed to bring the body into line. It is worth quoting Luther at some length to get his point here.

> Although, as I have said, a man is abundantly and sufficiently justified by faith inwardly, in his spirit, and so has all that he needs, except insofar as this faith and these riches must grow from day to day even to the future life; yet he remains in this mortal life on earth. In this life he must control his own body and have dealings with men. Here the works begin; here a man cannot enjoy leisure; here he must indeed take care to discipline his body by fastings, watchings, labors, and other reasonable discipline and to subject it to the Spirit so that it will obey and conform to the inner man and faith and not revolt against faith and hinder the inner man, as it is the nature of the body to do if it is not held in check . . . works reduce the body to subjection and purify it of its evil lusts, and our whole purpose is to be directed only toward the driving out of lusts. Since by faith the soul is cleansed and made to love God, it desires that all things, and especially its own body, shall be purified so that all things may join with it in loving and praising God. Hence a man cannot be idle, for the need of his body drives him and he is compelled to do many good works to reduce it to subjection.[16]

Luther cannot resist reminding his readers not to trust in works for their justification, yet he still insists that discipline, progress and order are needed, precisely because we have bodies. We have a physical nature alongside our inner life, which tends to work habitually. Our bodies need to learn different habits and be brought under control.[17] Left to themselves they will tend to keep wandering off the track, and so the body needs to be retrained to behave in accordance with its new nature. It is like someone who has corrective surgery after many years of walking with a stoop due to a twisted spine. Afterwards she might take time to learn how to walk upright again. The root problem has been solved, but the body needs to relearn how to act and move in accordance with the new reality.

To use another image, Luther says that faith is a bit like health. Just as good physical health is the precondition for profitable activity, in the same way faith is the essential precondition for good works.[18] With good health you can do most things. Without it you can hardly do anything. Faith in Christ provides the basic precondition for growth towards holiness, so that all the effort and energy put into the Christian life is properly effective, rather than damaging. It is a bad idea to try physical exercise while injured. If you pull on the weights machine with a fragile, slipping disc in your spine, or run on the treadmill with a weak hamstring, you are far more likely to do damage than to become fit. In the same way, trying to become virtuous while thinking that our salvation depends on it leads to a dangerous self-absorption, or an anxious, fraught pursuit of personal holiness, where the focus is not upon the other person who needs help, but on myself who needs to become good. It becomes self-centred, introspective and serious. In short, it takes the fun out of it.

In another place, Luther put the same idea slightly differently. He wrote about 'two kinds of righteousness'. The first is Christ's righteousness, an 'alien' righteousness or goodness, which justifies us. The second is what he calls 'our proper righteousness'. This is our own goodness, a goodness or virtue that grows in us over time and flows from the first kind:

> This righteousness goes on to complete the first for it ever
> strives to do away with the old Adam and destroy the body
> of sin . . . This righteousness follows the example of Christ
> in this respect and is transformed into his likeness. [19]

This kind of goodness, the kind that is nurtured in us by grace, is brought about by the process of order, discipline and structure, or as Luther puts it, 'slaying the flesh and crucifying the desires with respect to the self . . . in love to one's neighbour, and in . . . meekness and fear towards God'.[20]

Spiritual disciplines are not a betrayal of grace. When put in their proper place they protect it, strengthen it and help it work its way through a person's life. Imagine a growing tree: the life of the tree courses through the membranes that channel life from the roots to the leaves. But the tree also needs the bark to protect and guard that life, to keep it flowing and bearing fruit. Without the bark, the sap would either drain away to the ground or dry up as soon as it appears. In the same way, disciplines help protect the life of the Spirit and keep it flowing out into all the different parts of a person's life, rather than fading away or drying up.

Did Luther endorse the third use of the law? No and yes. He did not say that Christians need constant reminding of the exact shape of the Christian life, with detailed instruction on what to do and what not to do. He was wary of legalism at this point, fearful that Christians might start thinking that God liked them the more good works they did. Like the New Testament authors, he was no casuist. Christians need to hear about grace and faith more than they need instructions on what to do. But he did see and recommend the use of particular spiritual disciplines and practices to root out sinful habits, remind us of the word of grace and help us to grow in Christ-likeness. He saw these as vital for daily growth in Christ-likeness.

Motivation for goodness

Later in his life Luther became quite distressed by the low level of Christian life in the churches that claimed to be reformed. He began even more strenuously to insist on the need for order and discipline. Responding to stories of 'Lutherans' (although of course he hated the term) who drifted along, living lazy, careless lives because they thought they had faith, he warned of presumption. Freely chosen structures and devotional practices are to be encouraged, 'yet the people are to be taught that the only reason for keeping these festivals is to learn the Word of God'. Disciplines are needed to ensure that the word and grace of God are kept hidden in the heart and work themselves out in practice, in everyday normal behaviour.

Luther, however, never quite succeeded in finding a strong enough motivation for Christians to do this work of growing in goodness, realizing in their own lives the goodness of Christ which had become theirs by faith. Perhaps the reason for this was the Reformation's lack of an explicit theology of mission. It has often been noticed that the gaping hole in Reformation theology was any strong idea of evangelism or outreach. There are hints, but not much real reflection on it. Both Catholics and Protestants tended to relate growth in holiness to the doctrine of salvation. Catholics said that we should grow in holiness because our salvation depends on it. Protestants (or at least later Calvinists) said that we should grow in holiness as a way of proving that we are saved, or 'elect'. Turning to the Bible, we find a quite different and clear motivation for Christian behaviour:

> Let your light shine before men, that they may see your
> good deeds and praise your Father in heaven. (Matt. 5.16)

> Live such good lives among the pagans that, though they
> accuse you of doing wrong, they may see your good deeds
> and glorify God on the day he visits us. (1 Pet. 2.12)[21]

Christian goodness, or spiritual fitness is developed not primarily for our own sake, but for God's and other people's. This is one of the fundamental differences between the gym and the church. In the gym we are pedalling away trying to build physical health and fitness so that we will feel better, live longer and enjoy our lives. Even the more holistic 'mind, body, spirit', world essentially offers the motivation of feeling more peaceful, centred and in tune with ourselves. In the kingdom of God, however, the motivation is different. The question of our own salvation, security or value has been settled by the goodness or righteousness of Christ. Cultivating virtue is therefore undertaken so that God is glorified in us, and so that others are drawn to him.

The Christian who learns generosity, kindness or humility as a way of life begins to be noticed. Her friends and neighbours quietly begin to wonder why she seems different, striking, at peace. Some are offended and angered by what they assume is some kind of spiritual superiority; some are drawn to ask the question of why she is like this. The result is the glory of God and the salvation of people. If such virtue is absent, the non-Christian wonders what all the fuss is about. If Christians don't live in any discernibly different way from all the others, then why should he believe what they say? But if they do live differently, then it challenges, provokes and intrigues. Christian virtue is, at the end of the day, a missionary imperative.

This is a crucial point to grasp. The true motivation for growth in spiritual fitness is not that we feel better. It is that God is glorified in us. As Christian people and communities learn a new way of life, become capable of remaining patient, faithful and generous despite everything life throws at them, that begins to provoke questions, which of course leads on to fruitful evangelism.[22] It is only when growth in holiness – spiritual fitness – is placed in this context as the key to mission, that it finds its proper place, and stops leading us back into an anxious search for salvation through our own efforts, leading to the spiritual equivalent of constantly stepping onto the scales to check whether we really are losing weight or not. The work of Christ frees us from that. It makes us relaxed, joyful, at peace. It also encourages us to pursue spiritual fitness not for our own sake but so that others see it and are drawn to the Christ who inspires it.

Notes

1   Stanley Hauerwas and Charles Pinches, *Christians among the Virtues: Theological Conversations with Ancient and Modern Ethics* (Notre Dame: University of Notre Dame, 1997), p. 115.

2   Karl Barth, *Church Dogmatics,* trans. Geoffrey Bromiley, *et al.*, 4 vols. (Edinburgh: T & T Clark, 1957), II.2, p. 645.

3   J. J. Pelikan, H. C. Oswald and H. T. Lehmann, eds, *Luther's Works,* vol. 44 (Fortress Press: Philadelphia, 1966), p. 300. (Henceforth 'LW'.)

4   WATR 2.192.14 – 193.2. Quoted in D. R. Janz, *Luther on Thomas Aquinas: The Angelic Doctor in the Thought of the Reformer* (Wiesbaden: Franz Steiner, 1989).

5   WA 36.29.

6   See Gilbert Meilaender, *The Theory and Practice of Virtue* (Notre Dame: University of Notre Dame, 1984), Chapter 5.

7   LW 32.208f.

8   LW 32.229.

9   LW 25.260.

10 LW 37.365.

11 Meilaender, *The Theory and Practice of Virtue,* p. 126.

12 LW 31.361.

13 The issue was sharply debated at the Lutheran Eisenach Synod of 1556. Supporters of Melanchthon ('Philippists') were in favour of this third use, and the 'Gnesio-Lutherans' were against it. The Philippists won. See William H. Lazareth, *Christians in Society: Luther, the Bible and Christian Ethics* (Minneapolis: Fortress, 2001); Timothy J. Wengert, *Law and Gospel: Philip Melanchthon's Debate with John Agricola of Eisleben over Poenitentia,* R. A. Muller, ed., *Texts & Studies in Reformation and Post-Reformation Thought* (Grand Rapids: Baker, 1997).

14 *Treatise on Good Works* (1520), LW 44.21–114, p. 27.

15 LW 31.343.

16 LW 31.358f.

17 He makes similar points nearly 20 years later, during the antinomian controversy. See 'Against the Antinomians', LW47.107–119.

18 LW 44.34.

19 LW 31.300.

20 LW 31.299.

21 Of course Jesus also says in the Sermon on the Mount, 'Be careful not to do your acts of righteousness before men to be seen by them' (Matt. 6.1). The apparent contradiction between this and Matt. 5.16 can be resolved by considering the motivation for letting such behaviour become visible. In 5.16, Jesus recommends that good deeds should be made visible so that they may 'praise your Father in heaven'. In 6.1 he counsels against such public action with the aim 'to be seen by men'. The question is, who is glorified by good deeds: God or me?

22 See Graham Tomlin, *The Provocative Church* (London: SPCK, 2002), for a development of this key idea.

Chapter 7

The church and transformation

So how does it work? How can churches become centres of spiritual health and fitness? Has the church ever successfully done this? Are there models we can follow? Are we in danger of taking the church off down a track it has never trod before, with no map to follow? Or have we found a track that leads us back onto the main highway, back to the direction we should have been heading in all along?

As the saying goes, 'the past holds the key to the future'. As we start to ask the question of how this might work out in practice, we could do worse than look backwards to times when the church grew significantly, to find patterns that we might imitate in our own time. The most striking of those examples comes from the earliest churches themselves. The early centuries of the Christian church saw it expand at a remarkable rate across the Roman empire. They must have been doing something right! Not surprisingly, it was a period when the church took this task of spiritual fitness with great seriousness. Can we find a pattern there to help us today?

Early Christian formation

In the second century Irenaeus, a theologian based in Lyons in France, wrote that 'the glory of God is the living man, and the life of man is the vision of God'.[1] The one thing that shows the glory of God on earth more than anything else is when a human being becomes fully alive as always intended, reflecting the glory and nature of the Creator. That is where we can glimpse God before our very eyes. God became man, so that we might display his glory. Central to early Christian theology was the process of formation in which we are shaped into the image of God in Christ. A century later the Greek theologian Athanasius took the stage. He insisted against huge opposition throughout his lifetime that the church should hold to the belief that the divine *logos* or Word, who became incarnate in Jesus the Christ, was not created but part of God himself. When we say in the Nicene Creed, the most important early Christian statement of belief, that Jesus Christ was 'eternally begotten of the Father, God from God, Light from Light, true God from true God, begotten not made, *of one being with the Father*', we are reciting something which Athanasius clung onto with all his might, and which was hotly debated at the time. It may seem a fairly obvious part of Christian belief to say that 'Jesus is God', but the core of that simple statement was disputed. It made sense to say he was in some way 'divine', like some of the previous emperors, but how divine was he? Did he just bear a particularly strong likeness to God, or was he made out of the same stuff as God? Was he identical with the Father or different? If he was different, how could he still be God? And did it matter?

Athanasius argued that when the first humans fell, the image of God that had been placed in the human race was tragically and profoundly fractured. Although originally endowed with God's image, pure and undefiled, now that sin had entered the world two fatal changes had taken place. Humans had now lost their close, intimate knowledge of God, becoming ignorant of him. As a result they began to worship all kinds of lesser beings (this is Athanasius's explanation of the origin of pagan worship of the Greek gods). Second, they became subject to corruption and ultimately death: 'Man, who was created in God's image and in his possession of reason reflected the very Word Himself, was disappearing, and the work of God was being undone.' The result of this was obvious to him: 'Adulteries and thefts were everywhere, murder and rape filled the earth, law was disregarded in corruption and injustice, all kinds of iniquities were perpetuated by all, both singly and in common.'[2]

Athanasius was convinced that our fundamental human problem was not so much moral but natural. It is not just that we do bad things and need to sort ourselves out. There is a flaw in our nature; corruption has entered into humanity. It is as useless to say to a man 'be good' as it is to say the same thing to a rotten apple. Humanity, like decomposing fruit, was once pure and good, but is now far from what it might have been. Salvation is not just a matter of trying a little harder to be good. Something more than forgiveness is needed. Forgiveness is vital and significant, yet it only does part of the job. It is simply absolution from past errors and does not address the tendency to do bad things in the future or the fundamental problem of a corrupt and damaged nature.[3] Similarly, repentance alone could never be enough precisely because the problem is not our behaviour but our nature. The basic problem is that we have lost God's image and likeness.

So Athanasius sets up the 'divine dilemma'. What is God to do? His creation has been spoilt. Is he to screw it up, throw it away and repent of the idea of making a world altogether? No, he does the only thing he can do to rescue humanity – he restores the divine image in them, like a painter carefully redrawing an image that has become damaged and defaced. And he does it by sending his own Word, his *logos*, in human form: 'What else could he possibly do, being God, but renew his Image in mankind, so that through it men might once more come to know Him? . . . It was He alone, the Image of the Father, who could recreate man made after the image.'[4] In Athanasius's famous phrase: 'He became man, that we might become God.' The purpose of the incarnation was that humankind would again become like God, full of grace, truth, goodness and love. Imagine contracting a degenerative disease that slowly and inexorably will lead to death. Then imagine a doctor coming to inject an antidote that stops the process of decay in its tracks and reverses it, so that health comes flooding back into the body. That is what Athanasius means by the idea of the image of God being restored to humanity through Christ. This reversal of the process leading to death is appropriated when believers put their trust in Christ.

In other words, Athanasius holds so tightly to the idea of the incarnation not to satisfy logical consistency in doctrine or out of some abstract loyalty to an intellectual proposition. He does it because it provides the way for human life to be profoundly transformed.

This full doctrine of incarnation opens up the possibility of real human transformation. It offers the prospect that something can be done about human behaviour. Thieves, murderers, rapists, or even simple liars and cheats like most of us, can be changed and learn a new way of life through the power of God. As Rowan Williams puts it:

> Only God can 'deify', only the unequivocally divine saviour can decisively transform our lives, only the creator can re-create. The distinctiveness of the Christian identity is bound up with the idea of a 'new creation', of an event that makes a radical, decisive and unforeseeable difference in the human world: something is brought out of nothing, life from death.[5]

Athanasius's convictions came into conflict with some ideas developed by Arius, an Alexandrian priest, and those who followed him, who in their turn insisted that God was unique, could not share his nature with any thing or person, and therefore the Son must be part of creation, not part of God. The Council of Nicaea in AD 325 had condemned Arius's teaching, maintaining that Christ was 'of one being' with the Father (the Greek word was *homoousios*, a word which the Arians were unable to accept. Later on, a compromise solution was suggested, that the Son should be said to be *homoiousios* with the Father. The addition of that single letter, the Greek 'iota', changed the meaning from 'of one being with the Father' to 'of like being with the Father'. This was unacceptable to the orthodox, and they dug their heels in. Did it matter? Could one Greek letter really be worth such hassle? And if it was, why? What difference could it possibly make?

The difference, according to Athanasius and his followers, was that if the Son is only 'like' the Father and doesn't share his very nature, then the divine image cannot be restored to humanity, salvation cannot happen, and real profound transformation cannot take place. 'How . . . can the Son create in us what has to be created in him?'[6] Here was a case where a letter kills. The addition of that one letter was disastrous, because it meant losing the insight that God really does break into human life and salvation, that we can be remade in the image of God as we were always meant to be, that we can become like God again, showing his glory as Irenaeus saw. For Athanasius, there is an unbreakable connection between knowing God and a good life. True knowledge of God leads to right behaviour, and a good life is vital to knowing God – the two interact with each other in an indissoluble relation, a kind of spiral of growth. As we learn the true nature of God and the physical world, we become less possessive of material things and more willing to be generous with them. As we learn to do that, we know more intimately what God is like from imitating him from within.[7] For Athanasius, as for many other early Christians, the whole point of God becoming human was that we might be reformed into likeness to God, so that we might become images of God and imitators of Christ.

Early Christian instruction

Since the eighteenth century, theology has often seemed a rarefied academic pursuit, safely tucked away in universities, aiming at precision of explanation and clarity of thought. From its early days, however, Christian theology was a practical art, or at least a discipline focused on developing a better way of life. As the American theologian Ellen Charry puts it in her admirable book on this theme:

> . . . the classic theologians based their understanding of
> human excellence on knowing and loving God, the imita-
> tion of and assimilation to whom brings proper human

dignity and flourishing . . . [they] held that knowing and loving God is the mechanism of choice for forming excellent character and promoting genuine happiness.[8]

Charry's point is that the purpose of Christian theology in the classic Christian tradition was not just the definition of correct belief for its own sake, but the cultivation of virtue and excellence at the art of living. Theology was inextricably linked with Christian life, so that fine shifts in theology meant big changes in life. It was important to get the theology right, because when you get it wrong you end up living wrong. Instruction in good theology was vital for Christian formation of character.

How did that process of formation happen? One of the most important institutions in the early church was the catechumenate. As the church grew during its early years, many outsiders became interested. It had to devise a way of screening those who looked in. Those who were casually intrigued had to be weeded out from those who were serious about the new faith. The church needed to be protected from dilution by members who had little idea of what being a Christian meant. The catechumenate, a series of classes to introduce the Christian faith to enquirers, was the early church's means of ensuring that new Christians knew what they were letting themselves in for. Before Athanasius's time, the catechumenate played a pivotal role in Christian initiation. Those interested in Christianity, perhaps those who had heard a Christian speaker and been convicted by the sermon, were not expected to pray a prayer and 'become Christians' on the spot. Instead, they would join the ranks of the catechumens, those being taught the way of Christ in preparation for baptism, the point at which they would enter the Christian church properly. Clement of Alexandria tells us that the catechumenate in that particular north African city lasted around three years, although of course it varied from place to place.

The content of catechesis was a mixture of doctrinal, moral and spiritual teaching. Catechumens would be gathered together for instruction as part of the community celebrations early in the morning. The basic requirements of Christian life were laid out, spiritual disciplines recommended and the basics of Christian belief explained. Generally speaking, the process continued through various stages leading up to baptism, with personal examinations at the end of each.[9]

A document now known as the *Didache* (literally 'The Teaching'), usually thought to have originated around the end of the first century, is a brief account of early Christian exhortation, probably used as a guide for catechumens. It gives us a glimpse into early church teaching on Christian life and behaviour. The first thing to notice is that it describes Christianity not as a philosophy or a set of ideas, but as the 'Way of Life', as opposed to the 'Way of Death'. The characteristics of these two ways are not so much intellectual as moral – they are not primarily to do with what you believe, but how you live (although, crucially, how you live is seen to depend on what you believe). Christians will give generously when asked. They will avoid magic, astrology, abortion and sexual promiscuity. Masters will speak gently to slaves; slaves will respect and obey masters as representatives of God. Christians will avoid entertaining lust, wanting to be rich or feeling hatred for people, however bad those people might be. The reason for such behaviour is always linked into Christian convictions about God. We are created as social beings, called to love God our Maker and those he has placed near us as much as we would instinctively love ourselves. Christians are to be generous not simply because of an arbitrary command, but because this reflects God's nature, 'for it is the Father's pleasure that we should share His gracious bounty with all men'. The reason why masters are to treat slaves gently is that they are people 'whose trust is in the same God as yours'.

This small, early Christian guidebook for life offers clear rules for what Christians do and don't do, yet it is more than an instruction manual. The Christian is to put herself in the places where these qualities of love, generosity, honesty and self-control can be cultivated and learnt. She is to attend closely to those who bring the word of God to her. Fasting and confession are expected parts of Christian discipline. She is to 'frequent the company of the saints daily, so as to be edified by their conversation'.[10] Close association with the lives of those who are on this path is vital – exposure to other believers who are examples of Christian life to be imitated is an essential part of Christian learning. The goal is 'spiritual improvement; because all the past years of your faith will be no good to you, unless you have made yourselves perfect'.[11] The last word here does not mean perfection in the sense of flawless purity; it rather carries the connotations of 'maturity'.[12]

The invitation to the Christian life here is an invitation to growth in spiritual perfection. The *Didache* does not envisage a static life for Christians – it entices them into the process of learning a new way of life through exposure to the Word and Spirit of God.

We get an idea of what went on in later instruction of catechumens through the catechetical lectures of Cyril of Jerusalem during Lent in the year AD 348, delivered in the great new Church in Jerusalem, built over the (probable) site of the tomb where Christ was laid. For Cyril, catechesis is a process of refinement and transformation:

> Let your mind be refined as by fire unto reverence; let your soul be forged as metal; let the stubbornness of unbelief be hammered out; let the superfluous scales of the iron fall off, and what is pure remain; let the rust of the iron be rubbed off and the pure metal remain.[13]

Cyril seems to be ushering these nervous new potential recruits into a journey where they will be tested, purified and prepared for the dramatic new status which baptism will bring. He works his way through basic Christian doctrine, so they are in no doubt as to what Christians do and don't believe, and the way of life that is to flow from such belief. He also wants to try to arm them with material to fling at opponents who will inevitably challenge their new faith: 'You have many enemies. Take to yourself many

darts, for you have many to hurl them at: and you need to learn
how to strike down the Greek, how to contend against heretics,
Jews and Samaritans.'[14]

His talks to the newly baptized take things further. He runs
through the means of sustaining Christian life (fellowship, sacra-
ments, worship, etc.) and warns them not to go near the smutty
decadence of the theatre, the cruelty of the chariot races or
degrading pagan worship.

The early Christians clearly thought that the process of Christian education was vital to ensure a distinctive church. To keep the
church's radical edge in a non-Christian society meant a process of
teaching so that new Christians understood what Christian life
was and what it wasn't. By combining basic doctrinal instruction,
moral guidance and spiritual practices and disciplines, these new
recruits could be taught a new way of life which would mark them
out in their setting, whether for persecution or praise.

Early Christian community

Another aspect of the process of formation was gathering for
worship and Christian interaction. Writing towards the end of the
fourth century, Gregory of Nyssa, one of the great Cappadocian
Fathers who had a large influence on the church's emerging
orthodoxy, took Athanasius's theology of spiritual perfection
further still into a theology of spiritual aesthetics. Gregory shares
with 2 Peter, Irenaeus and Athanasius the sense that the goal of
the spiritual life is to be reshaped in the divine image. For him the
purpose of reading the Bible is not just to gain information about
God, but to learn how to conform to his nature:

> But one thing the sacred text should teach us is that . . .
> those who are to be initiated into the secret mysteries of this
> book must no longer be mere men, rather they must be sub-
> stantially transformed by Christ's word into something
> divine.[15]

One of Gregory's key insights is that we become like the things we worship. Pagans who worship the capricious and unpredictable Greek gods, with their tales of lust, jealousy and anger, become in turn capricious, unpredictable, lustful, jealous and angry. Those who worship the statues of the gods simply become dead, stiff and immobile like the static idols to which they offer devotion. On the other hand, 'those who look towards the true God receive within themselves the characteristics of the divine nature'.[16] The soul is like a mirror, which takes on the exact likeness of whatever it contemplates. So the soul is to spend time in contemplation of God, and this is the key to human transformation: 'Human nature . . . cannot become beautiful until it draws near to the Beautiful, and becomes transformed by the image of the divine beauty.'[17]

The church is the arena where this all takes place. It is the place where Christ can be found and worshipped, and therefore the place where both people and creation are restored to what they were always meant to be: 'The establishment of the church is a recreation of the world.'[18] As they take part in the community called church, and as they see and imitate Christ in each other, Christians are to be gradually perfected towards the likeness of God their Creator – although of course full perfection is impossible in this life. In fact, the kind of perfection true to humanity is found in movement towards the goal: 'Human perfection consists precisely in this constant growth in the good.'[19] As this process takes place, a life of virtue initiated by baptism progressively washes away the filth which sin has poured over the divine image in us, and likeness to God shines out again from human nature.[20]

Despite his mystical language, Gregory doesn't imagine the ideal Christian as lost in spiritual wonder, gazing at the divine in some numinous ecstasy. Likeness to God has very practical and social consequences. Becoming like God means sharing in his qualities, exhibiting the divine virtues, acting like God. It means humility, goodness, self-control, love and peace. The result is a change of character, like a garden blooming with flowers as the sun shines and the rain falls upon it.[21]

One of the chief ways in which this process happens is through the observation and imitation of other Christians. Gregory's language is bold and direct: 'He who sees the Church looks directly at Christ.'[22] What he means is that we see Christ in those people who have been shaped by years of following him, and we learn Christ by observing and imitating them.

Gregory's spiritual theology envisages a constant growth towards God, which begins with baptism, destroys sin and gives life. Christian living is then simply acting out what has happened in baptism, a delightful exploration of the landscape of divine love and grace to which baptism is the gateway, the point of entry. Here, at the heart of early Christian thinking, we find a powerful and transforming blend of theology, spirituality and ethics. The whole scheme centres on the idea that Christian life and worship consist of a gradual process of becoming like God, a process which grace and the community of the church make possible.

Early Christian discipline

Discipline also played a crucial role in the development of Christian character. In the third and fourth centuries after Christ, a growing number of men and women began dropping out of urban life to start living in the deserts of the Nile Delta, Palestine and Syria. They did so mainly in pursuit of a more radical form of Christian discipleship. Christianity was becoming just a bit too comfortable and easy in the cities. Being Christian was increasingly a sign of respectability after Constantine had made it central to his plans for the empire. In these desert-based communities was to be found a largely lay movement of people seeking more deep-rooted transformation in their own lives and society in general. They did so paradoxically by withdrawing from that society to a life of intensely focused prayer, Bible reading and manual labour, mostly lived together.

In the literature of the monks, the gymnastic metaphor crops up frequently. They saw each other as spiritual athletes, running after a very specific goal and in need of focused training. Euthymius, the founder of Palestinian monasticism, 'through daily athletic contest . . . built up self-control as regards the tongue and the belly, perfect freedom from possessiveness, true humility and sanctification of the body'.[23] Theodoret of Cyrrhus, a fifth-century bishop and a chronicler of the early Syrian monks, saw the whole monastic effort through the metaphor of physical, athletic contest. He described the strange array of characters in his 'Religious History' as 'athletes and gymnasts of virtue'.[24] He even describes a certain Eusebius of Telada, a leader of a group of monks in the desert who trained many others in the disciplines of the monastic life, as a kind of personal trainer. Writing of Eusebius's pupils, he says:

> Such victorious contestants did the divine Eusebius, the gymnastic trainer of all these contests offer to God. There are very many others who he formed like this and sent to be teachers in other wrestling schools, who have filled all that holy mountain with these divine and fragrant pastures.[25]

For Theodoret and many others like him, the monks of the desert had embarked on a journey of spiritual transformation, which could be likened to the preparation athletes made for the games. They were involved in a match not against physical opponents, but against spiritual ones – destructive, sinful desires which tugged away at the heart and drew their attention away from God. Taking their cue from St Paul's language of struggling 'not against flesh and blood, but against the rulers, against the authorities, against the powers of this dark world and against the spiritual forces of evil in the heavenly realms' (Eph. 6.12), they aimed at a form of spiritual fitness which would enable them to win this spiritual wrestling contest. As a result, they seemed to become capable of regular acts of goodness and virtue. Theodoret relates stories of monks who offered endless hospitality from their meagre resources, embraced their enemies, spoke with crystal-clear wisdom and tamed wild beasts, not to mention the many stories of miraculous healings and deliverance from demons. It is as if this spiritual vigour equipped them to perform tasks which others could not, just as physical fitness enables us to do things which would otherwise be completely beyond us.

We sometimes think of the monastic life as deliberately shunning all contact with the outside world. Yet there is a definite and deliberate tension in the accounts we read about these early monks. On the one hand, they aim to seek God with all their heart and attention, getting away from any distraction or temptation that might deflect them from that goal. The secret of spiritual power is loving God with all the heart, soul, mind and strength, paying rapt attention to him. On the other hand, they want their spiritual resources to be made available to others. So hospitality and the offering of wisdom and advice to visitors are crucial parts of desert ministry. And, in particular, evangelism flows. One story tells of how some thieves visited the cell of an elderly monk and promptly took everything he had (though it could hardly have been a great haul). Seeing that they had missed a purse that was hanging up in the cell, the old man chased after them, telling them to take that as well. Seeing this astonishing display of generosity they turned back, returned everything they had stolen and turned to Christ. Here was a man who had learnt such freedom from the need to possess things, that he was willing to give even to those who were his enemies. The stories of the monks are full of such encounters, where pagans, backsliders and miscreants of various kinds are converted by encountering the distinctive and selfless virtue of these radical Christians.

Many early monastic stories sound very strange to modern ears. These feats of asceticism, such as weighing themselves down with chains, living in walled-up caves, refusing to lie down, eating only leaves and denying themselves sleep for weeks on end, all sound just a bit crazy. In fact, the monks in Palestine often frowned on the extreme antics of their Syrian counterparts further north as a kind of spiritual showing off. However, that does not take away from this model of a transformed life through the exercise of certain disciplines, which in turn leads to effective evangelism, because it provokes questions in the minds of those who encounter such radical difference. The monks were seen as exercising a more extreme form of discipline than was available in the cities, yet the basic idea remained the same. Through a life of order, self-denial and focus upon God and his Word, sin could be gradually pulled up by the roots and virtue won. As others saw that, they could not help but be impressed and intrigued. Here was a vision of spiritual fitness, the acquisition of the kind of life that could not help but draw attention in a world searching for meaning and goodness.

Early Christian inspiration

All this on its own was not enough, however. Grace was needed, flowing through all human activity and effort, if true likeness to Christ was to be created. The great St Augustine, Bishop of Hippo AD 395–430, was one of the massive shapers not just of Christian thought, but of Western spiritual and psychological identity. His ideas have been controversial, but it is hard to dispute the effect they have had upon the way most of us think. For Augustine, the world's problems can be traced back explicitly to a primeval act of disobedience against God. As Cardinal John Henry Newman later put it, 'The human race is implicated in some terrible aboriginal calamity. It is out of joint with the purposes of its creator.'[26] Through the sin of the first humans, evil entered the world, affecting not just humanity but nature itself. Sin affects people in two main ways. One was what Augustine called 'Original Sin', by which he meant the guilt which every human being inherits at birth by virtue of being born into a race which carries the taint of sin. The other, 'Actual Sin', referred to the sins we commit from day to day. The primeval rebellion of the human race against our Creator leaves us both guilty and damaged. We remain under the sentence pronounced on a race which is guilty, but at the same time we are, as it were, spiritually and psychologically impaired in the process, so that we inherit not just guilt but an inbuilt tendency to do bad and destructive things to each other, to the created order and to ourselves.

For Augustine, God's answer to the tangled, twisted effects of sin is grace. And grace works on us in two main ways. First, it remits sins, removes guilt and wipes the slate clean. That kind of grace (operative grace, as Augustine called it) is received through baptism. More complex, however, is the grace that gradually removes the deeper effects of sin upon our wills, minds and actions. While it pardons and removes original sin, baptism only begins a much longer process that works on the presence of actual sin in human life.

At its core, sin affects the human will: it makes us want the wrong things. Augustine described this in his *Confessions* while recalling a childhood act of theft: 'My desire was to enjoy not what I sought by stealing but merely the excitement of thieving and doing what was wrong . . . It was foul, and I loved it.'[27]

Augustine saw the nub of the problem in the desire to find happiness in the wrong places: 'They choose to look for happiness, not in you, but in what you have created.' We think we can find security and joy through fame, sex, wealth, even other people, things good in themselves, but which can never fully satisfy. Only God can satisfy the hunger of the human soul. By infecting our desires, it also twists our minds, so that we no longer think straight. Our desires pull our thoughts along with them so that we no longer see the world clearly or in perspective, and we madly rush after dreams which can never fulfil us, things which, if we thought about them coolly, we would never imagine could make us happy.[28] The problem is that we can no longer think coolly about these things. This also works out in our behaviour: we desire the wrong things, think they will satisfy us, and so we do anything to get them, even if it means trampling on our neighbours or friends.

As a result we are all morally and spiritually disabled. We are deformed, twisted, no longer free to choose what is right, true and beautiful. We are as free to choose goodness and reject evil as a heroin addict is to turn away from his habit. We cannot choose to break free – we are in need of something much stronger. We need divine help, divine grace.

This kind of grace (Augustine called it cooperative grace) gradually frees us from the hold of sin over our wills, minds and behaviour. It does so by kindling within us a desire for God, the one who alone can make us truly happy and fulfilled. Slowly, cooperative grace frees us to love God and all that is good, and we begin to lose our passion for what is destructive and evil. As Augustine put it, 'God heals us, not only that He may blot out the sin which we have committed, but, furthermore, that he may enable us to avoid sinning.'[29]

For Augustine, while spiritual perfection is impossible in this life, growth towards it is possible. Grace, God's goodness breathed, or 'inspired' in us, gradually frees the will to desire God. It fights against the tug of sin and places within us a contrary desire, which longs for God and to be fulfilled in him. As that gathers strength, so the damage done by sin is healed and 'as we progress, our spiritual health keeps pace'.[30] Augustine insists that the primary mover in this process is not our effort, but God's grace – a vital distinction if we are not to lapse into an anxious, self-motivated and self-generated activism.

Augustine encouraged Christians not just to thank God for what he had done for them, but also to enjoy God. Holiness grows as we learn to enjoy, appreciate and practise goodness, justice, peace and compassion – the qualities of God himself. Through this process of spiritual formation we come to share the image of God once again. As Ellen Charry describes it:

> Christ is the model whereby the divine traits of justice, love, wisdom, and so on are taught to believers so that they taste and enjoy God directly, and thereby are transformed or conformed to God intellectually, emotionally and morally.[31]

Summary

The early Christians saw the vital first step of forgiveness and pardon, represented in baptism, as the beginning of a long work of God in the human soul. Christian formation, restoring the image of God in humanity, lay at the heart of salvation. The catechumenate insisted on a combination of doctrinal, moral and spiritual teaching as vital for keeping Christians on this track. Gregory of Nyssa pointed out the centrality of Christian community for the moulding of the human person. The monastic tradition put in place patterns of discipline – the means by which transformation might take place. Augustine emphasized the work of grace, the divine work in the human heart, as the key element in the transformed life.

If we are to build churches today that are capable of cultivating Christian character, these basic elements will still be necessary. The next chapter explores how they might work out in church life today, and how they can contribute to the development of spiritual fitness, the creation of people who can be entrusted with power.

Notes

1   Robert M. Grant, ed., *Irenaeus of Lyons, The Early Church Fathers* (London: Routledge, 1997), p. 153.
2   Athanasius, *St Athanasius on the Incarnation: The Treatise De Incarnatione Verbi Dei*, trans. A Religious of CSMV (London: Mowbray, 1982), pp. 31–2.
3   Alvyn Pettersen, *Athanasius*, Brian Davies, ed., *Outstanding Christian Thinkers* (London: Geoffrey Chapman, 1995), p. 67.
4   Athanasius, *On the Incarnation*, p. 41.
5   Rowan Williams, *Arius: Heresy and Tradition* (London: Darton Longman & Todd, 1987), p. 240.
6   *Ibid.*, p. 240.
7   Pettersen, *Athanasius*, pp. 80–2.
8   Ellen Charry, *By the Renewing of Your Minds: The Pastoral Function of Christian Doctrine* (New York: OUP, 1997), p. 18.

9   See Michel Dujarier, *A History of the Catechumenate: The First Six Centuries*, trans. Edward J. Haasl (New York: Sadlier, 1979).

10 Andrew Louth, ed., *Early Christian Writings*, Penguin Classics (Harmondsworth: Penguin, 1987), p. 192.

11 *Ibid.*, p. 197.

12 The Greek word used here is τελειωθητε, which carries the meaning of 'maturing' in New Testament writings.

13 Cyril of Jerusalem, 'The Catechetical Lectures of St Cyril', in *Nicene and Post-Nicene Fathers* (Oxford: Parker, 1894), p. 4.

14 *Ibid.*, p. 3.

15 Herbert Musurillo, ed., *From Glory to Glory: Texts from Gregory of Nyssa's Mystical Writings* (Crestwood, NY: St Vladimir's Seminary Press, 2001), p. 154.

16 *Ibid.*, p. 184.

17 *Ibid.*, p. 186.

18 *Ibid.*, p. 273.

19 *Ibid.*, p. 83. This is a radical departure from the Platonic tradition, which claimed that perfection was ultimately static. For Gregory, perfection was found in this constant movement towards God, which can never plumb the divine depths, never reach the point of having 'finished with God'. See Frances Young, *From Nicaea to Chalcedon: A Guide to the Literature and Its Background* (London: SCM, 1983), p. 117f.

20 Musurillo, ed., *Gregory of Nyssa's Mystical Writings*, p. 101.

21 *Ibid.*, p. 189.

22 *Ibid.*, p. 272.

23 Cyril of Scythopolis, *The Lives of the Monks of Palestine*, trans. R. M. Price (Kalamazoo: Cistercian Publications, 1991), p. 8.

24 Theodoret of Cyrrhus, *A History of the Monks of Syria*, trans. R. M. Price, *Cistercian Studies Series 88* (Kalamazoo: Cistercian Publications, 1985), p. 126. See also p. 133.

25 *Ibid.*, p. 56.

26 From 'Apologia pro Vita Sua', in Ian Ker, ed., *Newman the Theologian: A Reader* (London: Collins, 1990), p. 209.

27 Augustine, *Confessions*, trans. Henry Chadwick (Oxford: OUP, 1992), p. 29.

28 Sexual desire became for Augustine a picture of the kind of overpowering passion which blots out all other more rational considerations.

29 Augustine, 'On Nature and Grace', in P. Holmes and R. E. Wallis, eds, *Saint Augustine: Anti-Pelagian Writings*, vol. V, *Nicene and Post-Nicene Fathers* (Edinburgh: T & T Clark, 1887), p. 131.

30 G. R. Evans, *Augustine on Evil* (Cambridge: CUP, 1982), p. 161.

31 Charry, *Renewing*, p. 136.

Chapter 8

The church and the gym

For the early church, the context for Christian transformation and the development of virtue was not the classroom or the library, but the church. Just as modern gyms are dedicated to the physical health and fitness of their members, so the early church was focused on developing the spiritual health of those who became part of it. What shape would a Christian community take today if it was built around this goal, aiming to build spiritual health and virtue in each of its members, making them capable of exercising power without abusing it? This chapter begins to spell out what this means, by relating the five key elements which we saw in the last chapter to vital elements of church life today.

Formation

Lounging on the sofa watching TV and eating pizza will not usually make our bodies a picture of fitness and health. Lasting change normally involves the exertion, pain and discomfort of physical exercise, where we push ourselves beyond our bodily ease and comfort.

As the early Christians saw, a similar pattern applies in the spiritual life. Formation into likeness to Christ is central to the church's mission, and one of the chief ways in which God does that work of transformation in us is through something few of us want – suffering.

'Consider it pure joy, my brothers,' says James, 'whenever you face trials of many kinds, because . . . the testing of your faith develops perseverance' (Jas 1.2). One of the main themes of Scripture is the way in which God uses what is poor, unwanted and despised to fulfil his purposes for the world (1 Cor. 1.26–29). Suffering is usually unwanted and despised. Yet as James points out, it is usually through times of struggle and difficulty that God shapes us, rather than times of ease and comfort.

Michelangelo is reported to have said that he would choose a block of stone that felt as if it had the final statue hidden inside. His job was to reveal the beauty inside the rough stone, to chip away at it until, for example, the human form we see in his famous statue of David, was revealed. His chisel and hammer were merely the tools he used to bring out this perfection of form.

As James describes it, it is as if 'trials of many kinds' are the tools God uses to form in us the qualities needed to display his glory in the world. Trials, or the testing of faith, produce perseverance, a classic virtue required for the Christian to come to maturity, 'complete, not lacking anything' (Jas 1.4).

It is hard to escape the conclusion that God does not do his work in us apart from the experience of suffering and pain. If we are to develop the virtues that reflect the glory of Christ, that make us truly human and show the glory of God to the world, then the easy life will not do. It will never be enough to stay in our comfort zones, happy with doing our religious duty in private while living a quiet, contented life. That does not mean we are deliberately to invite problems and trouble. Nor does it mean that God inflicts trials or pain or suffering upon us. Just as he is insistent that God uses the experience of suffering to build virtue in us, James is equally insistent that such suffering does not originate in God: 'When tempted, no one should say, "God is tempting me." For God cannot be tempted by evil, nor does he tempt anyone' (Jas 1.13). For James, trials and struggles usually come from our own evil hearts, not from the will of God. Nonetheless, these experiences are the very things God has chosen to use to shape us into maturity. In a remarkable way, God turns the very things that deface and damage his image in us – sin, suffering and pain – into the instruments that reform us into his image.

If this is true, then churches will need to be places where such trials and tribulations can be openly admitted, dealt with and learnt from, rather than avoided and shoved under the carpet. Too often we expect church to be a place of harmony, peace and cooperation, and we are surprised when it is not. We also expect Christian life to be plain sailing and trouble free and think that God has abandoned us or doesn't like us when we hit sickness, bereavement, failure or disappointment.

A church that is serious about becoming a centre of real spiritual fitness and health will not try to hide difficult experiences. Nor will it depict Christian life as always characterized by triumph and success. That only leads to struggling Christians feeling inadequate and far from the centre of God's purposes in the world. I remember in my early years as a Christian leader talking to a woman in our church who had struggled with depression. I suggested that coming to church might help. 'Oh no, I couldn't do that – it would be much too difficult,' she said. 'When I get over it, then I'll be able to face church.' I could understand her reluctance to face the crowds of people, yet something about that didn't sound right. Whatever 'church' was in her mind, it was not somewhere you could take difficulties. It was instead a place for people who coped with life.

Church needs to be the opposite: a place for people who cannot cope with life. It needs to see itself as a place for people who know they are broken and damaged, spiritually flabby and unfit, needing to work through their troubles towards the maturity God wants to produce in them. It also needs to be open about the problems it experiences in its own life, the conflicts, arguments and misunderstandings, seeing these not as rude interruptions to its normal life of peace and tranquillity, but as creative opportunities for God's transforming grace to be at work, renewing us into Christ's image. It is the reality of the church as it is, a bewildering mixture of delightful grace and ugly conflicts, which is the very arena of God's work for spiritual health. It is through that kind of church, not the ideal one of our imagination, that God chooses to work. As the German theologian Dietrich Bonhoeffer wrote:

God will not permit us to live even for a brief period in a dream world . . . Only that fellowship which faces such disillusionment, with all its unhappy and ugly aspects, begins to be what it should be in God's sight, begins to grasp in faith the promise that is given to it . . . A community which cannot bear and cannot survive such a crisis, which insists on keeping its illusion when it should be shattered, permanently loses in that moment the promise of Christian community.[1]

Only such a positive acceptance of the experience of suffering and the existence of conflict can enable us to learn Christian virtue.

A key place where this is established is leadership. Churches tend to take on the personalities of their leaders, and where the leadership is invulnerable, distant and sets a tone of constant success, it may prove difficult for anyone else to admit to difficulties and open themselves to God's precious work through them. That doesn't mean leaders have to bare their souls constantly and wallow in failure. It simply means setting a tone where it is OK sometimes to struggle or to fail, in the knowledge that those are often precisely the ways in which God does his work of formation in us.

Instruction

Before you sign up for a gym, you will have been subtly or not-so-subtly indoctrinated. You will have seen the pictures of the athletes, the beautiful bodies, the hints and tips in health magazines that sell the story of physical fitness we looked at in chapter 2. It is essential we buy into this story, believe it and see how we fit into it – whether we are overweight and flabby, semi-fit, just needing a little body tone, or muscular and fit and just in need of maintenance – if we are ever to get started.

The same is true spiritually. As the early Christians believed, and as they practised through the catechumenate, we need to learn the story. We need to learn to think of ourselves not as secular liberal societies tell us we are – independent, autonomous consumers, voters, earners or taxpayers, but as the Bible tells us we are – created, beloved sinners, redeemed and called to bear witness together in the church to the kingdom of God and the lordship of Christ. Christian teaching will be a crucial aspect of the cultivation of virtue, because virtues always arise out of a story in which we participate: 'The individual virtues are specific skills required to live faithful to a tradition's understanding of the moral project in which its adherents participate.'[2] Those who begin an exercise programme need a clear idea of the goal – the kind of body they are aiming at. In the same way, Christians too need to know what they are aiming for as well, having a good under-standing of Christ, who he is, why he matters, and why and how they are to become like him. People wanting to develop Christian virtue will need to be immersed in the Christian tradition.

The kind of immersion needed here requires a wider set of practices than listening to a 15-minute talk every Sunday morning, just as the early church put in place a wider process of instruction than Sunday worship. There is a need for a more widespread and systematic programme of Christian education than we are used to. Christians need to know the story of the Bible and the basic outlines of Christian beliefs about humanity, God, the world, society and destiny. In previous ages, catechisms provided basic instruction in Christian faith. It is hard to see how churches can really expect their members to begin to develop the habits that grow out of the Christian story without some regular instruction in basic Christian doctrine. Courses such as Alpha have now become a regular part of many churches' lives and pro-grammes in evangelism. There is an urgent need to develop similar forms of teaching that go beyond Alpha to build this kind of basic Christian understanding and to develop the 'renewal of the mind' of which St Paul speaks in Romans 12. This means taking the disciplines of study, the public reading of Scripture (1 Tim. 4.13) and the private reading of Scripture, with great seriousness. It will also involve the deliberate memorization of

Scripture, either through passages learnt or through songs sung in worship. As Luther says, 'We should be so well versed and instructed in the Word of God that we have it at hand daily in all trials and will be able to strengthen ourselves and others.'[3]

Developing spiritual fitness will also require teaching that explicitly makes the connections between Christian theology and Christian virtue. This is a point made with much strength by philosophy professor Dallas Willard:

> It is not enough, if we would enable Jesus' students to do what he said, just to announce and teach the truth about God, about Jesus, and about God's purposes with humankind. To think so is the fallacy underlying most of the training that goes on in our churches and theological schools.[4]

Bob Lupton, a wonderful and inspiring Christian historian and community developer, once visited the theological college where I taught and asked the simple question, 'What are the most important commandments'? He got the answer he was expecting – to love God and to love our neighbour. 'So I assume,' he then asked with mock innocence, 'that those are the first classes you take when you come here?' There was an awkward silence. Like every other programme in Christian education, we did classes in biblical studies, church history, liturgy, ethics and the like, but nowhere was there a class on 'doing the things Jesus told us to'.

It sounds so obvious, but the absence of such a body of instruction is striking. This kind of teaching will not just consist of a list of instructions – that would be to fall back into a kind of unhelpful, barren legalism. Instead, it will aim to uncover the tight connections between theology and ethics, faith and life, and show how the one leads to the other.

To take an example, consider the doctrine of creation. When discussed in Bible studies or sermons, talk of the first few chapters of Genesis tends to raise issues such as evolution, science, the environment, or cosmology. There is, however, another way of seeing the doctrine of creation: as a tutorial in the art of generosity. Out of nothing, God creates a world. He did not need to, but he chose to make a universe, with our world as part of it. He made a space for us to live, flourish and find joy. He creates a rich, fertile, growing, immensely varied world which we could never completely explore even if we lived a thousand years. Creation is an exercise in generosity. It is an exercise in self-giving, outflowing goodness which seeks to bless others, and in which God himself finds pleasure. We are taught this under-standing of the world not just so that we might understand our origins or be thankful to God, but so that we might learn to imitate his lavish generosity in our relationships – so that we might become like him.

Dallas Willard writes:

> When do you suppose was the last time any group of
> believers or church of any kind had a meeting of its officials
> in which the topic for discussion and action was how they
> were going to teach their people actually to do the specific
> things Jesus said?[5]

So often Christian teaching and instruction never gets this far. Listening to it might be like going to hear a talk on the impor-tance of physical fitness, and going home again, never having to flex a muscle or shed a calorie. It remains at the level of ideas, mildly interesting but giving little real help in living well. If Christian faith really is intended to lead to the living of a new kind of life, then putting in place such forms of teaching – what Willard calls a 'curriculum for Christ-likeness' – is vital.

Such teaching can be done in other ways than just regular preaching. Imagine a course of classes that was designed to teach people to be generous, humble, patient, kind and to love their enemies. Imagine a church that advertised with all seriousness to its local community that it could teach them how to forgive, to trust, to conquer anger, to love their husbands, wives or children, or how to live joyfully, just as a gym offers to build muscular tone or shape our bodies. Such an offer might just draw in those who would never darken the doors for a more regular evangelistic outreach. In the 'Great Commission' at the end of Matthew's Gospel, the first part, 'making disciples of all nations', only really happens when the second part: 'teaching them to do everything I have commanded you', is taken seriously. Church members who are themselves experiencing change for the better, finding a growing capacity for mercy, love and generosity, are much more likely to invite their friends to be part of it than those who are stuck, feeling little real progress or development in their lives.[6]

Community

Gregory of Nyssa thought that transformation happened in community as we gather to worship God and to watch and learn from each other. When I first went to my gym, I was given a fitness test that told me which bits of my body needed working on. I was then given a list of exercises to do. The list didn't mean a great deal. What on earth was a 'lateral bend' or a 'single knee pull'? A 'dorsal raise' sounded more like something a dolphin would do rather than me. What I needed was someone to show me how to do it. So a young man who looked much fitter than I was came forward to show me what each of these exercises actually looked like. I guess if some flabby, overweight person had taken me through the exercises, I would have been less inclined to follow him. Yet because it was someone for whom these practices had clearly worked, I was more likely to try to imitate him, to copy the shape his body made while doing the various moves, in the hope that by doing so I would end up looking something like him.

A key part of our growing and learning, not just physically but also spiritually and morally, is by imitation. We watch someone else who has a quality we both lack and admire, and we learn to act and behave like them. I see someone who is particularly kind, and I think it would be good to become more like that, so I watch them, the individual acts of kindness they perform, and I start to do similar things myself. Virtue is learnt not simply by sitting listening to talks or studying books, but in normal human (or perhaps we should say Christian) interaction. To be in relationship with other Christians who are a bit further down the path of Christian life and practice is therefore vital if individual believers are to grow in Christ-like virtue.

Christian truth is always embodied truth, as it was in Jesus. Therefore we should expect that truth to be learnt as we watch it being enacted by masters of the Christian life. That is why in early Christian monasticism so much stress was placed upon the master, or 'Abba' (from which the title 'Abbot' eventually emerged). Learning Christian virtue came through a model of apprenticeship alongside catechesis, whereby beginners observed the life of those who had proved good examples to follow. Going back further, this explains why St Paul was able to say to the Corinthians, 'imitate me' (1 Cor. 4.16). He says it not out of arrogance, but out of the assumption in these earliest churches that imitation of experienced and settled Christians is one of the main ways in which Christian life and virtue are cultivated.

If imitation is a vital part of the way in which we learn virtue, then when Christians gather together, alongside space for worship and heartfelt, engaged praise, opportunities for interaction between Christians are essential, especially between relatively new Christians and more mature ones. Such interaction needs to involve more than just happening to be present at the same service, more than meeting for Bible study and prayer.

Newer Christians need regular exposure to the lives and habits of more tried and tested believers as a vital part of the learning of Christian virtue. There are two main ways this can happen. One is to ensure that as many people as possible belong to some kind of small group, a little like the Twelve who gathered around Jesus, which deliberately mixes the ages, placing younger Christians alongside those more experienced in the Christian life. Such groups will eat meals together, participate in local community projects, go on holidays, share in the bringing up of children, break the usual secrecy about the way money is spent.

The second way is through informal but committed mentoring. When I was a younger Christian, one of the most formative periods of growth in my life was when I was a regular visitor at the home of Mark, one of the leaders in the church I belonged to at the time. It was there that I learnt how a Christian uses their home and practises hospitality. I took note of the way he spent a little extra to insure his car so that he could loan it out to others to drive, and didn't seem that worried about the possibility of it getting damaged. I observed the way he would build relationships with some key younger individuals in the church to help disciple and encourage them. I watched the way he treated his wife and children, dealt with workmen who came into his home and reacted with calm when that home was burgled.

I realized that without knowing it (I had no idea I was being 'mentored' or anything as frightening as that) I had learnt a great deal because one older Christian had made it his business to include me in his life. Here is a vital task for those further on in the Christian life – deliberately to seek to bring younger Christians in on their habits, values, ways of spending time and relationship with their families.

If imitation is one of the ways we learn virtue, the training of our leaders will need to pay as much attention to issues of character and formation as to theological knowledge or practical skills. It would be little use having a gym instructor who knows the theory but is overweight and unfit. It is little use having Christian leaders who are theologically literate but show scant sign of humility, patience and self-control.

Earlier we noticed how the church is much more like a family than a bunch of friends. Families provide the vital context in which we learn how to act and behave in social settings through our formative years. Once you become a Christian the church becomes your new family, not replacing your old one, but welcoming you into a new, wider and more extensive family. The church can, however, only play a similar formative role if it enables something like the kind of exposure of life to life that a family does. So churches that are serious about becoming schools of virtue, communities that build spiritual fitness, will look carefully at how this kind of exposure can take place. Social interaction in church, whether harvest suppers, Bible studies, church weekends away or meeting in the pub with a few Christian friends, is far more than just social interaction – it is a vital way in which we learn the skills to live as Christians by watching, observing and imitating those we come to admire as good models of Christian life.

There is a place here, too, for the revival of Christian biography and autobiography. The church has always set great store by the art of spiritual 'lives', for example Athanasius's *Life of Anthony*, Augustine's *Confessions* and Adamnan's life of St Columba. These were vital tools in Christian imitation. By reading the stories of Christian lives lived well, those of us new to this path can begin to see what Christian virtue looks like, how character is developed and how it works out in practice.[7]

The point here is that change happens in community. It happens as we focus attention on God and as we learn what Christian life is from the other people in whom God is working. It operates in the combination of these two factors, worship and fellowship, which together make up community. If all we are engaged in is solitary worship, we do not have embodied contemporary models of Christian life to follow. If we have community but no worship, we have nothing distinctly Christian, nothing that can really form us in the image of God. It is by watching carefully both God and each other that we learn and change.

Discipline

A recurrent theme of this book has been the parallel between the physical disciplines that build bodily health and strength and the development of spiritual fitness. Our physical capacity is enhanced and advanced through specific exercises, and without a serious, determined approach it is likely that under the lure of tasty but fattening food and an indolent lifestyle our bodies will slowly deteriorate. It was taken for granted in early Christianity that certain disciplines were in place to enable growth in likeness to Christ. These were the disciplines of prayer, fasting, meditation on Scripture, study and the like. Alongside Christian teaching and Christian example, these were meant to be established as regular habits of life rather than occasional bursts of enthusiasm. It is no accident that the word 'disciple' is very close etymologically to the word 'discipline'. Disciples are made through disciplines.

This comes as bit of a shock in some Christian circles, either because of the Protestant misgivings about discipline examined in the last chapter or, more likely, because it all seems a bit too demanding. Few churches really engage their members with a serious programme of spiritual exercise or disciplines. As Stanley Hauerwas puts it, 'We have underwritten a voluntaristic conception of the Christian faith, which presupposes that one can become a Christian without training.'[8]

Yet training is needed, not for becoming a Christian, but certainly for living as one. In every other area of life where a new art or skill is to be acquired that does not come naturally to us, a programme of training is necessary. If you want to become really good at playing the flute, or golf, or building dry-stone walls, then the only way is to sign up for lessons and do lots of practice. Nothing less is true for the acquisition of Christian virtue.

The traditional Christian disciplines are usually divided into two lists: positive and negative, or disciplines of 'abstinence' and 'engagement'.

Disciplines of Abstinence	*Disciplines of Engagement*
Solitude	Study
Silence	Worship
Fasting	Celebration
Frugality	Service
Chastity	Prayer
Secrecy	Fellowship
Sacrifice	Confession
	Submission

What these are and how they are practised have been well covered elsewhere.[9] Here we will just make three points about them.

The first point is that the connections between such disciplines and the Christian virtues need to be clearly demonstrated. Sometimes it can be hard to see the value of fasting, confession or fellowship. Yet these practices are not virtuous in themselves – they lead to the cultivation of virtue when they are practised over time, which is vital for effective mission and evangelism.

Jesus expected his disciples to fast. He did not say 'if you fast . . .' but 'when you fast . . .' (Matt. 6.16–17). Fasting can, of course, be seen as heroic self-denial, fitting in with a view of the Christian life as essentially spiritual and otherworldly. This can lead people to think of fasting as an end in itself, detaching us from earthly pleasures. Yet this does not sit very well with the world-affirming nature of a faith in which God becomes flesh and which claims that he 'richly provides us with everything for our enjoyment' (1 Tim. 6.17). Clearly fasting for the Christian is not intended as a means of denying pleasure or detachment from the physical world. It is instead a means to an end. It is usually coupled in the New Testament with prayer and is designed to enable the singleness of purpose and purity of heart needed to 'see God', as Jesus put it in the Sermon on the Mount. For example, it was through fasting and prayer that the church in Antioch heard the voice of the Spirit telling them to set apart Paul

and Barnabas for a specific mission trip (Acts 13.1–3). Fasting
develops the ability to wait for God, to hear him speaking
directly as the church comes together to pray. In other words,
fasting is closely connected to the virtues of patience and atten-
tiveness. It is not meritorious, but it extends our capacity to pay
close attention to what God may be urging us to do in response
to his self-revelation in Christ and the Scriptures. It also develops
self-control, one of the central Christian virtues. An ability to say
no to something as small as an occasional meal is good training
for the ability to say no to much bigger things, such as the temptation to betray your friends or cheat on your wife or husband.
Occasional deliberate practice in saying no is a vital component
of a focused life in an indulgent culture.

In the same way, chastity, though not an immediately popular
discipline today, actually develops faithfulness and trust, qualities
that are essential in the building of healthy long-term relationships. Sacrifice builds generosity and kills acquisitiveness. The
discipline of worship cultivates love and inhibits self-centredness,
as we come to love God and all that is God's, including my
irritating neighbour or closest friend. Proper submission to those
in authority inculcates humility and puts an end to pride and
arrogance. Celebration leads to joy, and frugality brings self-
control.

Each of the classic Christian disciplines helps to develop Christian virtues. If these disciplines are to be built into busy
contemporary lives, however, the benefits will need to be made
clear. As such virtues become part of our regular habits of life,
reflecting the character of God in Christ, the result is a community of people who provoke questions in the minds of their wider
communities as they live out this radically new and distinctive
kind of life.

A second point is that these virtues themselves need practising.
Bearing in mind Luther's concerns about the relevance of Aristotle's moral philosophy for salvation, Aristotle has a point when it
comes to the establishment of the habits of virtue, for the sake not
of salvation but of mission. Patience, humility and gentleness

need to be practised. Habits are formed when practices become second nature to us – when we become so schooled in the story of Christian salvation and in the practice of the corresponding qualities of humility, patience and kindness that we exhibit them without even thinking about it. God is glorified not only when people profess faith but when they put it into practice. It is sometimes said that if you do something regularly, like brushing your teeth or combing your hair every day for a month, it becomes a habit that is harder to break than to give up. We are, as the saying goes, creatures of habit. Most of our regular practices and common reactions have come about through habitual actions, for good or ill. The art is to learn good habits, not bad ones; habits that are consistent with who we are in Christ and the purpose for which we are made. That is why teaching on the virtues has to include practice and not just theory, as we will see in the next chapter.

The third point is that very often the traditional disciplines have been seen as private affairs, and we have an image of the lonely spiritual athlete battling away in his or her cell to pursue this rigorous way of life. If all we have been saying in past chapters is true, however, then these, as well as any other aspect of the Christian life, have a communal dimension as well. It is difficult to maintain such habits for any length of time, or at least the length of time needed for them to make any discernible difference. This is especially true in a culture that does not generally see the value of long-term disciplines of life, whether of self-denial or positive action. One of the chief ways in which this can be overcome is by a mutual sense of accountability and encouragement. Of course there is the great danger that such practices are done to impress others, a tendency Jesus puts his finger on quite severely: 'Be careful not to do your "acts of righteousness" before men, to be seen by them. If you do, you will have no reward from your Father in heaven' (Matt. 6.1). Yet this does not necessarily mean that such disciplines have to be conducted entirely in secret. It is a healthy warning against showing off about spiritual growth, but it does not preclude the practice of such a way of life in fellowship with an intimate group of Christian friends to whom we let ourselves be accountable for our progress in the faith.

A movement such as Renovare offers a programme for the practice of spiritual disciplines in small groups, called 'Spiritual Formation Groups'.[10] Taking their cue from Hebrews 10.24, 'let us consider how we may spur one another on towards love and good deeds', movements such as the Benedictine monastics, the seventeenth-century Wesleyan Methodist 'cells' and the more recent Alcoholics Anonymous agree a covenant of confidentiality and mutual encouragement to help each other grow in ability to master destructive temptation and live well. Meeting regularly, such groups will provide a setting in which the joys and difficulties of practising the disciplines can be talked over and vital motivation to persevere can be found. A church can build a simple, manageable structure that enables intimate, accountable groups to encourage growth, just as groups of friends might visit the gym together, work out together and generally encourage each other along the track towards physical fitness.

Inspiration

Augustine saw that this work of transformation is essentially a divine, not a human, work. All of these elements on their own cannot produce spiritual health and fitness. There needs to be an explicit dependence on the Holy Spirit as the one who works transformation. A danger of the physical fitness metaphor is that it can suggest that we can manage and determine the process ourselves. Instruction, imitation, disciplines and trials are instruments and not sources of the virtuous life. There is, of course, no conflict between these and a dependence on the Spirit – the Holy Spirit usually uses particular means to do his work. That is why God gives us what have traditionally been called the 'means of grace': bread and wine, baptismal water, the Word read and preached, prayer, and so on. God tends to like to work through us and through such things rather than independently. However, churches also need ways of constantly expressing this ultimate dependence not on techniques or systems but on the Spirit of God. A trinitarian understanding of God's work of salvation demands such a perspective. The Father sends the Son to embody and reveal the divine nature. He descends to the very depths of the cross to redeem the creation from its sinful rebellion, and is raised from death to conquer the age-old enemies of humankind and make access to the presence of God possible for us sinful human beings. The Holy Spirit is the one who then draws us into fellowship with God by enabling us to respond to him. Without the Spirit, we are 'dead in our trespasses and sins' as Paul puts it, unresponsive to his advances, deaf to his voice. When the Spirit comes upon us, we suddenly find ourselves waking up to God, longing for his presence and likeness, and finding that very likeness growing within us as we walk by the Spirit.

The Spirit is the one who makes all this possible. He is like the life which courses through our veins, the basic energy which makes possible the exercise that develops physical fitness. Without him, all the effort would be at best a waste of breath, at worst impossible.

Churches taking this agenda seriously will need to retain expectancy for the Spirit's tangible and experiential work. Worship, prayer ministry, counselling and preaching that expect the Spirit to work in a direct and noticeable way will create a sense of openness to God's work, beyond our own capacities. They will regularly remind Christians in the church that this work of spiritual transformation is not a human thing, but a work of God himself. It is a work where God does as he always does: taking human structures, orders, means and practices and infusing them with life to bring about Christ-like character, attractive virtue and surprising joy.

As the church puts such things in place, it can begin to expect spiritual fitness to grow in its members. Teaching on the virtues, close encounters between older and younger Christians, structures that enable people to view the challenges in their lives as points of growth not frustrating obstacles, a programme of simple, manageable spiritual disciplines, all surrounded by a dependence on the work of the Spirit, will enable a church to retain this focus on being a place of growth. It will enable churches to become the kind of communities that genuinely demonstrate transformation and change, offering something of real and lasting value to people who otherwise might disdain it as unnecessary.

Notes

1 Dietrich Bonhoeffer, *Life Together*, trans. John W. Doberstein (London: SCM, 1954), pp. 15–16.

2 Stanley Hauerwas, *A Community of Character: Toward a Constructive Christian Social Ethic* (Notre Dame: University of Notre Dame, 1981), p. 115.

3 LW 42.55.

4 Dallas Willard, *The Divine Conspiracy* (London: Fount, 1998), p. 353.

5 *Ibid*, p. 345.

6 The next chapter will explore what this might look like.

7 The early church and early Middle Ages had a strong tradition of the use of Christian biography to inspire imitation and discipleship. Several examples are helpfully collected together in Carolinne White, ed., *Early Christian Lives*, Penguin Classics (London: Penguin, 1998).

8 Stanley Hauerwas, *After Christendom?: How the Church Is to Behave if Freedom, Justice, and a Christian Nation Are Bad Ideas*, 2nd ed. (Nashville: Abingdon Press, 1999), p. 98.

9 The above list is taken from Dallas Willard, *The Spirit of the Disciplines: Understanding How God Changes Lives* (London: Hodder & Stoughton, 1988). The book also contains a valuable discussion of these disciplines and their practice. See also Diogenes Allen, *Spiritual Theology: The Theology of Yesterday for Spiritual Help Today* (Cambridge, Mass.: Cowley, 1997); Richard J. Foster, *Celebration of Discipline: The Path to Spiritual Growth*, rev. ed. (London: Hodder & Stoughton, 1989), Richard J. Foster and Kathryn Yanni, *Celebrating the Disciplines* (London: Hodder & Stoughton, 1992).

10 See http://www.renovare.org.

Chapter 9

A masterclass in virtue

Jesus' public ministry lasted around three years. In that time he turned around the lives of a small group of people who then went on to exert a huge impact on the world. As we think about the practicalities of this vision of a community focused on the task of spiritual transformation, health and fitness, it is not a bad idea to ask how Jesus went about it. How did Jesus develop faithfulness, compassion or patience in the lives of his followers?

In other words, what if we were to take Jesus' ministry with the Twelve as a model for church? It is perhaps an unusual idea, but if church is essentially those who gather together around Jesus Christ, it shouldn't be such an odd thing for our attempts to build community to try to learn from the way that Jesus did it. In particular, if his time with the Twelve was so transformative for them, might it have something to teach us about how we build Christian communities capable of developing spiritual fitness? This chapter takes a close look at Mark's Gospel to sketch the way Jesus did church. It picks out twelve features, commitments or values which we might build into our churches as we try to turn them into communities as capable of spiritual and personal transformation as this small band of disciples in the first century.

Companionship

A striking feature of Mark's Gospel is that Jesus very rarely did things alone. Occasionally he went off into the hills to pray, but most of the time he did everything with his disciples. At times it was with the whole group, at other times he took just a few of them along, but he rarely acted alone. The pronoun used most often is 'they', not 'he'. As Jesus moved through Galilee, then on down towards Jerusalem for the climax of his ministry, this was a communal journey where everything was done together. They experienced together the elation of the transfiguration when Jesus took Peter, James and John with him on that most extraordinary and personal encounter with his Father (9.2–13). They experienced together the grief and despair of the death of Jairus's daughter (5.35–43). They encountered fear (4.38) and went through failure (9.18). Jesus took them through the whole range of human experience and they went through it together, not alone. There was a commitment to each other which transcended even commitments to family. In fact, this group actually became as close as a family – Jesus asks the rhetorical question, 'Who are my mother and my brothers? He looked at those seated in a circle around him and said, "Here are my mother and my brothers!"' (3.31–5).

As strong as their commitment to Jesus was their commitment to each other. Here at the heart of Jesus' practice of church was a willingness to expose his life to theirs and their life to each other's, in the intimate setting of a small community of around a dozen people. Without that depth of companionship, it is unlikely that our churches will get very far with real transformation.

Hospitality

Sometimes the most interesting features of a text are revealed in the asides, the incidental details rarely noticed. Mark 1.29 says, 'As soon as they left the synagogue, they went with James and John to the home of Simon and Andrew.' In 2.15 again, 'While Jesus was having dinner at Levi's house, many tax collectors and "sinners" were eating with him and his disciples.' They did spend quite a bit of time in each other's homes. To allow someone into your home is to allow them into your own private space. It is much more intimate and exposed than meeting someone on neutral ground like a church building.

When we enter a person's home, we learn much more about them than if we meet elsewhere, because homes reveal a great deal. Visiting a friend's home will tell me a lot about their taste in colours, music and decor, how they like to arrange their own private world and what their true values are. We might say blithely in church that we aim to live simply. Whether we really do or not will be quickly revealed by a glance at the way we decorate our homes and manage our possessions. Outside our homes it is easy to pretend, to hide. Inside, all is revealed.

When I was a young church leader, charged with looking after the youth group, the suggestion came up that this growing church might build a new extension. I was asked whether I wanted a specialist 'youth area' to enable the young people to meet in a central venue, rather than the existing practice of meeting in various church members' homes. The idea of a swish new youth venue had a certain attraction, but I still felt uneasy. The great virtue of taking these teenagers around various Christian homes in the parish was that they were able to watch older Christians in their actual places of living. They were able to study Christian hospitality in practice, and I sometimes even hoped that coffee would get split on the carpet so they could watch an older Christian respond without too much fuss and so (hopefully!) learn something about the true value of possessions and the virtue of hospitality.

Church buildings are valuable and useful, especially when churches become large. Yet they are not *necessary*. The earliest churches didn't have them and did in fact meet in homes. Hospitality was therefore a central value for the New Testament church, I suspect not just for practical reasons but also for spiritual and theological ones. Just as God welcomes us to his table, we are to welcome others to ours.

Meals

Jesus and his apprentices spent a lot of time eating. They visited Levi's house for a meal (2.15), the home of Simon the leper was another meal venue (14.3), and we know from the other Gospels that the house of Mary, Martha and Lazarus was a regular place where they would eat together. In particular, the Passover meal provided the setting for the most intimate moment of encounter between Jesus and his friends, where they not only shared each other's food, but even shared in Jesus' flesh and blood. In fact the only specific gathering Jesus told his followers to have was to gather around a meal. No morning service, prayer meeting, church council committee – just a meal with him and the rest of his followers.

Meals in the ancient world always signified far more than just physical nourishment. They were always a sign of acceptance and fellowship. You ate with your friends and family; you did not eat with your enemies. Even today, though such meanings are not so explicit in our culture, eating together is more than just re-fuelling. Meals play a crucial role in socializing us as people. They signify welcome and communion, as we eat with those we want to get to know better or already know well. Over meals we relax. We talk about what is on our minds, what is happening in our lives, deals we're involved in, family troubles, politics, sport, everything. It is where healthy families meet and talk about things that matter to them. They are less formal than meetings, less pressured than interviews. Meals provide a vital setting for the sharing of life, which is why they played such a key role in the relationship between Jesus and his friends.

Wasting time

Jesus and his friends also spend quite a lot of time not doing very much. If we didn't know better, we might say they enjoyed just wasting time together. Again it is the incidental details that reveal much. In Mark 2.23 we read how, 'One Sabbath Jesus was going through the cornfields, and as his disciples walked along, they began to pick some ears of corn.' In other words, they just went for a lazy walk together, during which the disciples roused the ire of the Pharisees by plucking grain on the Sabbath. They seem to wander from house to house, and it almost seems a nuisance when the crowds get so big 'they were not even able to eat' (3.20). Jesus takes them across the lake, during which a storm brews up (4.35). He crosses back over to the land of the Gerasenes (5.1). These journeys do not appear to have any particular purpose apart from spending time with the disciples. Not all of Jesus' ministry was focused, purposeful and intense.

Finding time is one of most difficult things in our busy lives. Yet building in this unhurried time spent walking, travelling, watching, talking is one of the most delightful as well as formative things we can do. Those times enabled the disciples to watch Jesus and imitate him. Did they pluck the ears of corn because that was exactly what Jesus was doing? Why else would they have done something so provocative unless he had done so first? Church that intends to become a centre for real spiritual change will always have an element of this gentle, unordered, though deliberately chosen policy of relaxed time together.

Practice

It was not all leisured ease, however. The friends of Jesus were sent out with specific tasks. They were told to heal, to preach, to drive out demons. Mark 3.14, the verse which tells us that they were called to be with him, continues with the further purpose of that calling: 'that he might send them out to preach and to have authority to drive out demons'. In 6.7 we find the same thing – the apprentices were sent out by the master two by two, taking minimal supplies, sleeping wherever they could find a welcome and telling people of the kingdom of God.

They were constantly being sent out from their warm fellowship with Jesus to do specific tasks, always things which Jesus himself did. He never asked them to do something he had not done first. They were sent to demonstrate the reality of the kingdom of God by preaching the message, healing the sick and driving out evil. This was the flip side of wasting time. It was very intentional. There was a conscious commitment to keep pushing themselves beyond their comfort zones, putting them in situations where they were out of their depth, where they would need to depend on God's power and presence if they were not to fall flat on their faces. The meeting where Jesus first told them they were to go out to heal, exorcise and preach was probably quite alarming. They were not trained preachers, healers or exorcists, simply fishermen, labourers, tax collectors. They must have felt very exposed. The meeting when they came back to report on what had happened when they tried it was much more upbeat (6.30). This was a constant feature of their life together – regularly taking on tasks together which bore witness to the kingdom of God and which took them into uncharted territory.

Our Christian gatherings also need elements of this if real spiritual fitness is to develop. Christians often gather for worship, Bible study, prayer, or to listen to talks. Mission trips or practical, active ministry projects that engage and challenge are equally important. Such things were a regular part of Jesus' work with his disciples. It stretched them in ways mere talk could never do. It built their relationships and enabled them to learn skills they used for the rest of their lives. Like the exercise undertaken in a gym, it changed them for good.

Retreat

The busyness of practical assignments and outward-focused ministry was punctured by times of retreat and rest. This was a little different from 'wasting time'. It was not slow, unhurried leisure, but deliberate reflection and rest together from the demands of ministry. In 6.31 Mark tells us that, after Jesus has heard all they had been up to, 'because so many people were coming and going that they did not even have a chance to eat, he said to them, "Come with me by yourselves to a quiet place and get some rest."'

This rhythm of practical ministry and rest, refreshment and reflection seems to run through the story. It doesn't happen all the time, but the narrative is sprinkled with evidence that this is what they did. Again, the church needs this too: a sense that we rest together, to reflect on what has been happening. A small group from the church I belong to recently went on a mission trip to Kenya. They each raised money for the airfare, did the mission work with the church they had linked up with, and then took a five-day holiday together on the African coast. Both ministry and retreat were done together, a crucial balance in developing a pattern of exposure of life to life, enabling imitation that leads to the learning of virtue.

Teaching

Jesus spent quite some time sitting down teaching, sometimes just with the Twelve, sometimes addressing a larger group. Yet the way he does it is not what we might expect from our normal experience of church. Mark 4 is a classic example. Jesus begins to teach by the lake. The crowd that gathers round him becomes so big that he has to get in a boat and go a little way off the shore to speak to them from there. He tells them a story. Subsequently, his disciples ask him to tell them more – to explain what it meant, as they didn't get it first time around. So it carries on.

Jesus' teaching took place not just in the initial 'sermon', but in the interaction of questions flowing back and forth. The disciples didn't just sit there, listening to the talk and taking notes, shaking Jesus' hand on the way out, saying, 'Nice sermon, Vicar.' They came back to him and kept on asking, 'What did that mean? Why did that happen? How does that work?' The questions were not just one way, though. Jesus asked them questions all the time. He taught as much through asking them questions as through telling them truths.

Just consider the number of questions Jesus asks the disciples in Mark 8: 'How many loaves do you have?' (v. 5) 'Why does this generation ask for a miraculous sign?' (v. 12) 'Why are you talking about having no bread? Do you still not see or understand? Are your hearts hardened? Do you have eyes but fail to see, and ears but fail to hear? And don't you remember? When I broke the five loaves for the five thousand, how many basketfuls of pieces did you pick up?' (vv. 17–19) 'Do you still not understand?' (v. 21). Then, of course, comes one of the key questions in the whole Gospel: 'Who do people say I am?' (v. 27) Even this question is intriguing. We might wonder why Jesus didn't say more obviously who he was. Why didn't he simply come out and say, 'I'm the Son of God, believe in me'? But that's not his way of teaching. His way of getting them to the point he wants them to reach is to ask them to work it out for themselves.

The other remarkable aspect of Jesus' way of teaching is his use of stories, parables which drew out thought and reaction. 'Then he began to speak to them in parables,' Mark tells us (12.1). If we take out the stories, we remove the guts of Jesus' teaching. Very often the stories didn't even have a 'moral'. They were simply left to work their magic in the minds of those who heard them, or were given a brief enigmatic summary: 'The first shall be last and the last shall be first,' or, 'For the Son of Man came to seek and to save the lost.'

Teaching in churches that want to reproduce Jesus' work with the disciples will aim to replicate something of this style of interactive teaching. This doesn't mean abandoning sermons (after all, Jesus did still preach), but they will not stop there. Such churches will build into their programmes regular opportunities for interactive learning, so that those who learn get the chance to quiz those who teach. Both end up learning more. And as a result, the story of Christian faith takes deeper root, leading as we have seen, to a life of Christian virtue.

Scripture

Jesus constantly returned to the Old Testament Scriptures as a central resource for his teaching. Many of the questions he asked the disciples took them back to the text of Scripture. 'Have you never read what David did?' (2.25) 'Why then is it written that the Son of Man must suffer much and be rejected?' (9.12) 'What did Moses command you?' (10.3). Jesus' teaching and ministry with them was a constant conversation with Scripture. Whenever a question was raised, Jesus seemed to go back more often than not to the Scriptures, whether it was about divorce, the meaning of his own life or events that were happening around them.

Jesus had been a regular at the synagogue since his childhood. He was known as a rabbi and therefore as someone well versed in the Scriptures. This says a great deal about how Scripture is to operate in churches that are serious about spiritual fitness: they will immerse people in the story of the Bible so that when questions emerge the natural instinct will be, as it was for Jesus, to ask, 'What do the Scriptures say?' This is not to claim that all the answers are lying on the page for all the different questions that will come up. Jesus' own use of Scripture was creative, interpreting it in ways that his contemporaries found shocking and new. Yet he never felt at liberty to dispense with it, and if our churches are to form people in a distinctively Christian way, then neither must they.

Observation

Jesus is often pictured just watching with his friends, observing what is happening around them and talking about it. In Jerusalem he loitered around with the Twelve, watching people on the way in. He noticed the rich unloading their wealth into the treasury and the widow dropping her tiny coin in as well (12.42). He drew their attention to the incident and they began a conversation about the real value of giving and sacrifice. They then noticed the huge stones that make up the temple itself, one of the disciples pointing them out this time. They then discussed the temple, its meaning and its future. A fig tree became the occasion for talking about God's judgement on Israel, and a child was an image of the order in God's kingdom.

Jesus encouraged in them a keen eye to observe what was happening around them, watching the world and learning to interpret it wisely in the light of the Scriptures. That was often the way Jesus used Scripture – to interpret the signs of the times, to discern the meaning behind events that were taking place in the natural or political or religious world. The skill of looking at the world differently, viewing it through the lens of Scripture, can be encouraged in Christian communities by deliberately practising it – taking items from contemporary culture or news and considering how we view them as Christians. Developing this skill builds the capacity to discern not just the Christian way of thinking, but the Christian way of acting virtuously in a secular culture.

The poor

Jesus' community showed a particular commitment to the poor and suffering. Simon's dying mother-in-law (1.29), the physically disabled (2.1–10, 3.1–6), the bereaved (5.21–43), the ethnic minorities (7.24–30), the blind (8.22) – these are the kind of people with whom Jesus and his students spent much of their time. The rich didn't appear very often in the story. The rich young ruler did make an appearance, but he sought out Jesus, not the other way round, and he was sent away with a lot to think about. The group did spend quite some time together, yet the focus of the group was not on itself, but on the world outside it and on exercising transforming influence within that suffering world.

There is a centrifugal force to this fellowship that drives it from its secure and intimate base to engage with the world around. The life they develop among themselves is not for themselves, but they deliberately seek out those whose lives are marked by struggle, pain and trouble in order to bring healing and relief.

It is remarkable when affluent, educated Christians begin to discover the difference they can make by using their skills to get involved in the lives of those who are very different from them. Bob Lewis's book *The Church of Irresistible Influence* gives an account of an American megachurch that discovered the liberation of turning itself around from a community that merely sucked people into its life to one that encouraged those very people to get involved with homeless projects, mentoring young offenders, or giving advice to unemployed job-seekers.[1] Again, the learning and benefit goes both ways. We set out with a commitment to those with whom we would not normally choose to spend time, but who need our skills, experience or help, and find so often that we are the ones who gain most. Qualities of compassion, patience and kindness, things we never felt capable of before, begin to emerge. Communities shaped by Jesus' way of doing church will experience this again and again.

Simplicity

The last value of Jesus' 'church' is simplicity of life. This group's manner of life was marked not by affluence but by a commitment to a gentle, uncluttered simplicity. 'These were his instructions: "Take nothing for the journey except a staff – no bread, no bag, no money in your belts. Wear sandals but not an extra tunic"' (6.8–9). This is not absolute poverty, but a simplicity that expresses dependence on God rather than financial security as the bedrock of a human life. They are to take not much more than they need to be able to operate within the particular society and culture in which they are seen to live and work. Presumably they are to give away the rest. This is not total ascetic abstinence. They do enjoy good food, wine, even the expensive perfume of the woman from Bethany (14.3). They enjoy life and the good creation God has given, not despising it as beneath them. Yet they are very careful in case affluence might shape their lives more than a basic dependence on God.

Jesus

This may sound an obvious place to end, but the point is still worth making. The centre of this small community was Jesus himself. Everything revolved around him. Wherever he went, they went. What he did, they did. The Twelve were apprentices, students of Jesus. Mark 3.14 says 'He appointed twelve – designating them apostles – that they might be with him.' That was their central calling: to be with him, to watch him, to live with him and learn from him. The whole point of them being together was to learn his way of acting, speaking, thinking, reacting, so that they could learn to do the same.

It is a simple idea, but easily lost. Over the centuries the church has developed into a hugely complex institution with its synods, buildings, canon laws and internal politics. It is good to remember that at its heart it is simply a group of people gathering around Jesus. He is the primary model of spiritual fitness and health, and he needs to be the focus of any Christian community. There are few prayer meetings in Mark's Gospel, but there is lots of talking to Jesus. In church, prayer can become a sonorous, self-conscious and serious matter. In the Gospels it was a simple communion with Christ, a habit of regularly asking him for advice, talking with him and being aware of his presence. That habit of simple, frequent, unfussy communion with Jesus has to lie at the heart of a church focused on learning his way.

There may be many more such values that can be drawn out from the story. Those included here are very briefly drawn. Yet the point is not so much the precise values themselves as a simple idea. If our churches are to become centres of spiritual fitness, communities in which people can find the means to be transformed, learning new habits of life and avoiding bad ones, they could do a lot worse than follow the pattern of Jesus and the Twelve.

When we begin to engage in this exercise of the imagination, we find a pattern of church that looks very different indeed from what most of us have experienced. Of course, Jesus and his disciples would also have attended the synagogue, the temple in

Jerusalem, and all the other activities of Jewish religion at the time. Jesus was no anarchist – he supported the religious institutions of the day, even if he could also be distinctly critical of them. Yet these twelve commitments – to companionship, hospitality, meals, wasting time, practice, retreat, teaching, Scripture, observation, the poor, simplicity and Jesus himself – reflect some of the key elements of his way of building community. Maybe they should also be reflected in our attempts to build the community of Jesus Christ today?

Can this work today?

Jesus spent three years full-time with the Twelve. Most of us have jobs, families, friends and commitments that make this exact way of life unworkable. However, it is not beyond the imagination to think of how Christian groups can operate in this way.

If I look at the main services on Sunday at the church I go to, I don't see many of these qualities – the gathering is simply too big to enable them to happen. There is teaching, the reading of Scripture, companionship with Jesus in heartfelt worship, but that's about it. I do, however, find these values in the small groups or 'pastorates' that make up the church. These are groups of around 20–30 people who meet fortnightly to live exactly this kind of life. They will always eat a meal together, do social things, 'wasting time' together like going to a movie or the theatre (or on holiday to Kenya like the group mentioned before). They might get involved as a group in a project in a local deprived housing estate, or discuss what is happening in the world or in the newspapers. They will read and study Scripture together and encourage a life of simple commitment to Christ.

It is only in such groups that this life can be lived. Whether they are part of a large church or an independent expression of church in a distinct culture doesn't matter. Whether you call them cell groups, home groups, base communities, pastorates or anything else doesn't really matter either. Attending Sunday services can never be enough. But neither need it take every minute of every day. A group that meets once a week and is serious about the kind of things Jesus was serious about can have a massive impact on a person's life. It can offer exactly the kind of formation, instruction, community, discipline and inspiration that enable change. In particular, such a group can enable exposure of one Christian life to another, leading to imitation of good models of Christian virtue, which has the power to build Christian character.

One of the key themes of this book has been that we learn Christian character by imitation. Of course, instruction, prayer ministry and spiritual disciplines are all important, but unless we have actual models of Christian life to copy, we are unlikely to be able to understand how these factors work out in the details of life. Jesus' work with the Twelve gave them an intimacy with him that enabled them to watch him, copy him and do what he did. They learned to preach, to heal, to care for the poor, even to walk on water, by watching him and imitating him. We badly need structures in our churches that facilitate such imitation. Groups of around the size of the one Jesus had, with a commitment to share lives, homes and resources, provide just that. They are an indispensable part of growing the kind of church that can develop spiritual health.

Note

1   Robert Lewis, *The Church of Irresistible Influence* (Grand Rapids: Zondervan, 2001).

Chapter 10

Learning goodness

The last chapter looked at imitation. This one looks at instruction. How might we learn to do all the things that Jesus commanded us to do? What would a 'curriculum for Christ-likeness' look like? We have seen the values a church needs to hold close to its heart if it is to develop Christian character. But how might we teach and learn the particular Christian virtues? There isn't space here to look at all of them, but I will take one and try to show how Christian virtue can be taught.

A large number of the intractable problems that face us both in our individual lives and in society can be traced to one thing: an inability to forgive. Whether it is a long-standing family feud or a national or tribal conflict, real or perceived insults and injuries lie festering away, gradually destroying our ability to relate. If we were able to let the past go, to forgive and no longer allow past harm or maltreatment to dominate our relationships, think what a difference that might make to our lives, and to the world. If churches were more capable of teaching people how to forgive, preventing small hurts from growing into large grievances, then they would offer something priceless to their communities – something that perfectly reflects the nature of God, who forgives freely.

What follows is the outline of a class on forgiveness. It starts with a suggested talk on the subject, then goes on to offer some ideas for homework, exercises that enable people to put into practice what is being taught. It ends with some general principles lying behind this approach to teaching virtue.

The necessity of forgiveness

A few years ago my parents were driving happily along the motorway, when steam suddenly began to seep from under the bonnet. They quickly turned onto the hard shoulder, looking down at the temperature gauge, to find not surprisingly that the dial was pointing dangerously to the red section of the scale. It was then that my father knew what had happened – he had been intending to get a small oil leak mended for some while, but had forgotten. The oil had now dribbled out and an engine always overheats without oil.

In a car's engine, hard metal constantly rubs against hard metal. Oil lubricates the parts so they do not become too hot and wear out. Forgiveness does exactly the same for human relationships. People rub up against each other all the time in families, workplaces and neighbourhoods. And occasionally friction results – things get overheated and strained. It is exactly at that point that forgiveness comes into play. Forgiveness enables us to get over misdemeanours which others cause, both real and imagined hurts that are inevitable unless you live entirely as a recluse. If I were to withhold forgiveness from anyone who offended me in the slightest, I would soon have few friends left. I would become trapped in my own unforgiveness and bitterness.

When I was a university chaplain, I remember talking to a girl who looked pale and thin, who was experiencing worrying symptoms of lack of sleep and loss of appetite. When we talked of what lay behind her illness, it became apparent that much of it stemmed back to her relationship with her parents. They had sent her away to boarding school at a very young age, which she then hated. Ever since she had blamed her parents for her unhappiness and feelings of rejection, and had been unable to extend forgiveness to them. It was only when she managed to forgive them from her heart that she began to heal inside, transforming her in every way possible.

However, it is not just at the personal level that forgiveness is needed. Some of the most intractable national or tribal conflicts can never move beyond stalemate, basically because of an inability to forgive. So easily a cycle of hatred and violence can build up, whether between Israelis and Palestinians, Hutus and Tutsis, Sunnis and Shi'ites. For many people in our supposedly civilized world, an inability to forgive is quite literally fatal.

One example that shows the contrasting power of forgiveness is the recent history of South Africa. That country is by no means a haven of peace and security, but the willingness of Nelson Mandela to offer leadership in not seeking revenge against those who had oppressed his people, and instead to forgive, enabled the country to move beyond the pain of the apartheid era towards constructive relationships between black and white. The 'Truth and Reconciliation Commission', set up to face up to and deal with the pain of those years, had as its specific mandate 'offering amnesty and forgiveness rather than punishment and dismissal'. Forgiveness gave South Africa the chance to escape the cycle of destruction. Archbishop Desmond Tutu, who led the commission, entitled his autobiography *No Future without Forgiveness*. He was absolutely right.

Forgiveness is not only necessary, it is also powerful. In 1980 the Italian Vice-President Vittorio Bachelet was murdered by the Red Brigade, an extreme left-wing terrorist group active in Italy at the time. At his televised funeral his son deliberately expressed his family's forgiveness for his killers. Years later, when some leaders of the Red Brigade were brought to justice, Bachelet's brother received a letter signed by 18 members of the terrorist group, inviting him to meet with them. They wrote, 'We want you to come – we remember what your nephew said at his father's funeral, that ceremony when life triumphed over death, and we too were overcome.' What police forces across Europe had failed so long to do, forgiveness achieved. Forgiveness has the power to break down barriers which seem impossible to breach; it can melt hearts of stone.

Forgiveness has the power to reconcile enemies and dissolve conflicts which lead literally to death. It also has the power to free both the forgiven and the forgiver. For it is not only the unforgiven who are held in bondage by a lack of forgiveness. Those who cannot forgive are just as bound as those who beg for mercy. To be unable to forgive is to be locked into bitterness that eats away at the soul. It is to be condemned to an ever-narrowing circle of dark, insatiable thoughts of revenge, a desire that consumes the victim until they have nothing left other than this aching need to cause as much pain to someone else as they once experienced. It is to experience a living hell.

To discover the power to forgive is to find real liberation, the ability to move on and leave behind the grip of pain or the desire to get even, which can never be fully satisfied. It is real freedom.

The difficulty of forgiveness

It may be necessary and even powerful, but forgiveness is far from easy. The phrase 'forgive and forget' trips off the tongue, but is in reality glib and shallow. Faced with something trivial, like the kids borrowing the car without asking, or someone treading on your toe by accident on the bus, then it is quite easy to forgive and forget. When someone has stolen your wife or husband, killed your child after driving while drunk, or told lies about you to your closest friends, it is much harder.

In 1978 the Egyptian Prime Minister Anwar Sadat shook hands with the Israeli Premier Menachem Begin. It was an act which symbolized forgiveness and reconciliation after years of bitterness and hostility. It also cost Sadat his life, as three years later he was gunned down by members of the extremist Egyptian Islamic Jihad movement.

Perhaps we can understand their depth of feeling. Forgiveness always seems scandalous, unfair or even immoral. It sometimes seems to minimize the crime or the suffering of the victims, even to suggest that it didn't matter. Forgiveness can seem a cheap way of dealing with profound and real hurts. One of Jesus' disciples once asked him how often he should forgive someone who keeps offending him. Once? Twice? Seven times? Jesus' answer is now famous: not seven, but seventy times seven – you keep on forgiving no matter how bad the offence is or how often it is committed.

Really? Can he be serious? Are Holocaust survivors to forgive their tormentors? Are parents to forgive the paedophiles who abused their children in so reckless a way? Are children to forgive those who deprived them of their parents for the crucial years of growing up?

There are two things to say at this point. One is that, as C. S. Lewis pointed out, there is a big difference between forgiving something and excusing it.[1] Excusing something means saying, 'It doesn't matter, it's not your fault – there is nothing to forgive.' Forgiveness, on the other hand, looks squarely in the face of injustice and wrong and says, 'Yes, there is something to forgive. It was your fault, it does matter and it did hurt. But I will never hold it against you, and everything between us will be exactly as it was before.'

Forgiving is also different from forgetting. That is vital to understand, otherwise we will feel that unless we can forget deep hurts which have caused us pain, we cannot forgive. What if, like the girl mentioned earlier whose parents had seemingly abandoned her, you cannot forget? Well, you can still forgive, because forgiveness does not say, 'I have forgotten.' Instead it says, 'I know what you did, and I remember it only too vividly. However, I choose not to let it come between us. We can still be friends. We can still stand together.'

The second thing to say is that forgiveness is far from cheap. There is always a cost involved. Forgiveness involves releasing a debt that has been incurred, and that always costs the one who forgives it. If someone owes me £1,000, and I choose to forgive that debt, it costs me. It means I have £1,000 less than I had a right to, and I will have to make do without it. In the same way, for a parent to forgive the drug dealer who led her child into addiction, or for a son to forgive his father's killers, seems impossibly hard. There are only two ways in which the pain caused by such a crime can be dealt with. One is revenge, the other is forgiveness. In revenge, I make the other person pay – I simply pass on my pain to someone else. In forgiveness, I choose to pay. I pay the price, and bear the cost myself by renouncing my right to recompense or justice. Both are costly. Forgiveness is only immoral if it really is cheap, if it fails to address the real costliness of reconciliation. What costs nothing is worth nothing. In fact, when we have deeply hurt someone, and we know it, we don't want a forgiveness which costs nothing. For someone to say, 'It doesn't matter, just forget it', can seem to cheapen the relationship, as if it is so shallow that it really didn't matter when it was broken.

That is at least part of the reason why, in Christianity, forgiveness involves atonement. Sometimes people ask why God cannot just forgive us and let it be; why does it need the bloody and messy business of Christ's sacrifice on the cross? One way of understanding this deep mystery is precisely this sense of the costliness of forgiveness. Forgiving human sin is not a cheap or easy thing. To forgive our deep crime against the order of the universe, our destruction of the beauty and harmony of the world God placed us in, is no easy business – it is a matter of life and death. What costs nothing is worth nothing, and for God to forgive us costs. He can either make us pay, or choose to pay the price himself. That is exactly what he does when he goes to the cross for us in the person of his own Son, Jesus Christ. He pays the price of our sins, not us.

The act of forgiveness

This insight opens up the way for us to begin to do something as difficult as forgiving. Corrie ten Boom was a Dutch woman whose father hid Jews from the Nazis during the occupation of their hometown, Haarlem, in World War II. Betrayed by one of their compatriots, the family were captured and sent to Ravensbrück concentration camp. Although several members of her family died, Corrie survived and, being a Christian, began to speak in many places of the way in which forgiveness was the only power that could heal the history of hatred in Europe.

One day she was preaching this message in a church in München. After the sermon a man came up to her, stretched out a hand and said, 'I'm so glad to have heard you, and that we can now be reconciled.' She instantly recognized him as one of the guards from Ravensbrück, one of the men responsible for the death of her beloved sister. She felt paralysed. Despite her words, should she, could she, shake his hand? All the memories came flooding back. It was one thing to talk about forgiveness. It was another to actually forgive. Instantly she prayed for forgiveness for her own lack of forgiveness. And instantly she felt the power to stretch out her hand to offer forgiveness and reconciliation. She knew she had the power to forgive this man.

The story illustrates the point: the key to being able to forgive is the realization that you have been forgiven.

In the Gospels we find two stories which make this point very vividly. One, told by Jesus, involves a king and two of his servants. The first servant owes a vast sum to the king. He is in massive debt – the equivalent today would be around one billion pounds – and faces ruin and destitution, both of himself and his family. Called into the palace of the king, expecting to be told he is to be sold into slavery or thrown into jail, he pleads for his life. Astonishingly, he is told that out of sheer mercy the debt has been cancelled, the account cleared, and he is a free man.

Overjoyed, he skips out of the office and makes his way home to tell his wife and children the good news. On the way home he bumps into a fellow servant who is also in deep debt, and who happens to owe him a small amount. He stops, his face turns from a smile into a scowl, and he demands payment from this second servant. When this man pleads for more time, the forgiven debtor insists that the other servant sells everything he has to pay his debt, leaving him homeless and destitute. When the king finds out he is, not surprisingly, angry and throws the first servant back into prison where he should have been all along.[2]

The story makes the point starkly and clearly. Once I have been forgiven a huge debt, it makes no sense at all to withhold forgiveness from anyone else. In fact, it is unnatural: if I do, it shows that I haven't been listening, or I am a deeply ungrateful wretch, or I think nothing of the price someone else has paid so that I can be forgiven. Put differently, if I know I have been forgiven a massive debt, then it becomes just that much easier to forgive other people who have hurt me in whatever way. The key to the ability to forgive is the knowledge that I have been forgiven.

The other story connected to the ability to forgive is a real incident in Jesus' life. He goes to dinner with a very religious man called Simon. When Jesus arrives, Simon omits all the customary marks of respect due to a guest, such as having his feet washed, offering him a kiss of greeting, and such like. It is as if you went to a party to find the host offering handshakes, taking the coats and offering a warm smile to all the other guests, but when you arrive he deliberately ignores you, leaving you to hang up your own coat and find your own way in. Somehow, a prostitute finds her way into the back of the gathering, and slipping to the front, she does all the things which Simon has omitted – kissing Jesus' feet and wiping them clean with her hair, which is all she has to dry them with. Simon is disgusted at this show of devotion by an unsavoury character and is about to have her thrown out of the house, when Jesus tells a story of two men who owe different sums to a moneylender, asking him which one will love the moneylender more. Simon answers, 'I suppose the one for whom he cancelled the greater debt.' 'Exactly', says Jesus. Simon thinks he has no sins worth speaking about to forgive. As a result his heart is hard, unforgiving, rude, full of contempt for people he thinks are worse than himself. The prostitute is only too aware of the depth of her sins, as she is reminded of them constantly by people like Simon. So when they are forgiven, as she no doubt has heard from Jesus before, she is full of gratitude, love, humility and grace.[3]

In the teaching of Jesus, God's forgiveness of us is always closely tied to our forgiveness of others. In the Lord's Prayer we are taught to pray, 'Forgive us our sins as we forgive those who sin against us.' It is the same thought that we find in these parables. When God forgives us, it is not just so that we might enjoy a new relationship with God and the freedom of knowing no guilt or shame before our Creator. It is also so that we might gain the ability to forgive other people. It is a tutorial in the art of forgiveness.

Christians are nothing more nor less than forgiven sinners. It is important to emphasize both of these words. We are *sinners* – we fail to put ourselves out for our neighbours as we should, let alone the poor on the other side of the world who need the resources that we squander on trifles such as cosmetics, DVDs and books. We lack generosity, we get angry with our families, we look out for our own interests before we ever think about those of others. In other words, our insecurities and lack of trust make us live in a self-oriented way, rather than a God-oriented or others-oriented way, as we were intended to. I may think I am not as bad as everyone else, but that is not the point.

At the same time, Christians are also *forgiven* sinners. Jesus' story of the king who forgave the debt of a billion pounds is his way of trying to help us see how much it costs God to forgive our sins. A sure way of measuring how big a debt we owe is to ask how much it costs to forgive it. If it cost the death of God's Son, then this can be no cheap deal. This is serious. But the cross tells us that God has paid that huge price. We are not excused, but we are forgiven.

Now if we are to learn to forgive from the heart and not just with a grudging reluctance (after all, only forgiveness from the heart has real power to change us and other people), there are several steps we have to take, which can be summed up in these words: Penitence, Prayer and Personal Contact.

Penitence
The first step is to face up to our own need for forgiveness. If, like Simon the Pharisee, I think I really don't have much to be forgiven for, then I am likely to find it hard to forgive others. Why should I when they fail to meet the standards I find easy to meet? That is the problem with nice middle-class religion which tells everyone that they are fine, decent and respectable, but which fails to mention the unfortunate and unfashionable subject of sin. It leads to a strict moralism which is hard to live with if you're a failure, and leaves people without the ability to forgive others. As Jesus puts it, 'Those who have been forgiven little, love little.'

We will need to examine regularly our own motives, actions and attitudes, being brutally honest in comparing them not to the low standards we see around us, but to the character of God reflected in the person of Christ. We need to admit that we are hardened, committed addicts to sin. We may not like to think of ourselves in this way, but unless we do we will find forgiveness difficult. The reason why we need to confess our sins regularly is not so that we should wallow in a pit of guilt, but so that we might experience the forgiveness of sins ourselves, and so become the kind of people capable of forgiving others. If we do receive the forgiveness that God offers, then we begin to become capable of real, costly, true forgiveness from the heart that has the power to heal relationships, our own hearts and even whole communities. As Paul put it, 'Bear with each other and forgive whatever grievances you may have against one another. Forgive as the Lord forgave you' (Col. 3.13).

Prayer
The second step is to pray for those who have hurt us. In the Sermon on the Mount Jesus says, 'Love your enemies and pray for those who persecute you' (Matt. 5.44). Prayer places the person we pray for alongside God in our minds and hearts. It enables us to begin to imagine how God sees them, rather than how we see them. As we pray for our enemies, those who have hurt us and whom we need to forgive, over time we start to view them differently. As we realize that God has no favourites, that he 'causes his sun to rise on the evil and the good, and sends rain on the righteous and the unrighteous' (Matt. 5.45), it begins to dawn on us that God loves this person, even if we don't. We begin to see them, not as the person who told lies about us, or betrayed our trust, but instead as the recipient of God's good and generous gifts, someone created and loved by God despite their destructive behaviour. When we add to that our sense of our own guilty, mean behaviour, we find our hard hearts beginning to soften, and forgiveness starts to become possible.

Personal contact

The final step is to talk to those we need to forgive – actually to make contact with them and offer forgiveness. Jesus continues in the Sermon on the Mount, 'If you greet only your brothers, what are you doing more than others?' (Matt. 5.47) Real forgiveness goes beyond staying with the people with whom we feel comfortable and just changing our own internal feelings. It goes beyond this to meet face to face with those from whom we are estranged, to extend forgiveness and make reconciliation real. It means making contact not in a condescending, patronizing way, but as one sinner to another, weak and poor, bound together by the simple fact that God extends his love and forgiveness to both.

Such a talk is only a part of the class. A number of other elements are crucial. The approach needs to blend Christian theology and actual practice. Without a strong foundation in Christian teaching such as the theology of forgiveness outlined above, it will quickly become another self-help class with its roots in pop psychology or positive thinking. It will lose its character as distinctive Christian behaviour rooted in faith and trust. It will soon become a strenuous and stressful exercise in self-development. It will also lead to pride. Growth in virtue that lacks an explicitly Christian motivation will tend to make us feel rather pleased with ourselves at having developed such abilities. It is only through keeping our feet firmly grounded in the grace which lies at the heart of Christian theology that freedom and real effective change can be maintained.

This is not just a pragmatic point. The centre of God's revelation is in a person, Jesus Christ. Although he also reveals himself in the words of Scripture and in the created order, the primary focus of God's self-revelation is personal. One of the results of this is that Christian theology never has a merely conceptual character. If Christian theology is a response to God's revelation of himself, in a sense it is impossible to do justice to it merely by discussing it in an abstract way in a classroom. If his self-revelation comes in personal form, embodied in the words, deeds, relationships and character of a person, then our response to it needs to take a corresponding form. If God had communicated to us solely or primarily in words, then perhaps it would be appropriate to respond to it only in words of discussion and analysis. Our response to God's initiative in revealing himself needs to correspond to the form of that self-revelation, if it is to be in any way appropriate or fitting – or, to put it differently, if it is to bring the sense of completeness, joy and freedom that it was intended to give.

As a result, it is crucial that this kind of teaching makes it clear that it is not a Bible study on forgiveness, not a study class, not even a prayer group. Its purpose is not to discuss the virtue of forgiveness, nor to explore its theological meaning or ethical or social implications. Its purpose is actually to teach people how to forgive. This is why it needs a number of other elements besides the talk.

Discussion and interaction

In a course on the Christian virtues, the talk would be delivered in the context of a meal, much as normally happens on an Alpha course. It would be followed by a chance to consider in groups what has been said. A number of questions might be suggested for discussion, such as:

- How do you feel when you are told that you are 'no more and no less than a sinner in need of forgiveness'?
- Is it true that 'the only way to learn to forgive is first to realize that you have been forgiven'?
- Have you ever experienced the power of forgiving someone, or being forgiven by someone?
- Is it ever right to withhold forgiveness?
- Should we forgive if the offender has not expressed sorrow for what he or she has done?
- Why is it sometimes so hard to forgive?
- In Tom Wolfe's *The Bonfire of the Vanities* the adulterous central character asks his wife to forgive him. She replies, 'I suppose I could. But what would that change?' Does forgiveness change anything?

- Is forgiveness immoral? Does it minimize the seriousness of the crime?

Practice

After each session, a number of practical actions would be suggested to give people the chance to enact what they have heard, to begin to build these practices into their lives as regular habits, not just occasional bursts of goodness. It is important that these are not compulsory, they are just suggestions.

So, for example, in the sphere of forgiveness, the group might be given the following as possible actions:

- Find a prayer of penitence and work through it slowly and carefully each day for a week.
- Make a list of all the people you have had difficult relationships with in the past – parents, siblings, teachers, work colleagues or neighbours. Pray for each one, asking for forgiveness for any lack of forgiveness in your heart and deliberately forgiving them anything they have done to you.
- Thinking of someone you find it hard to forgive, commit yourself to praying for them every day for the next two weeks.
- Write a letter to someone you have held a grudge against, offering forgiveness and reconciliation.
- At the end of each day, spend ten minutes thinking back over the day. Confess your own sins of that day and then, reflecting on any difficult relationships you have encountered, forgive those people in your heart.
- Rent out the video/DVD of *The Passion of the Christ* and watch it through, bearing in mind the thought, 'This is how much it costs God to forgive my sins.'

Of course no one is expected to do all of these. However, it might be suggested that everyone tries one which seems to fit their situation. There is no point in encouraging people to invent grudges where none already exist!

Follow-up

Each week of such a course would have a list of practical suggestions, such as the one given above about forgiveness. The following week it would be important to have a section at the start of the evening giving people a chance to talk about what they found when they began to practise these things. Did it make a difference? Was it hard or easy to do? How might you build this in as a regular habit of life? How can we help each other continue to grow in this particular Christian virtue?

Prayer ministry

The last chapter stressed the role of the Spirit in the cultivation of virtue. This is a work of God, not a human process. This too is vital, if it is not to be seen as a very self-oriented enterprise, depending on human effort and ability. So such a course would also need to build in the opportunity for prayer ministry with those who take part. A topic such as forgiveness will often raise deep feelings and memories, which have not been brought to the surface for many years. These need careful handling in the context of prayer. While some will need more professional help and expertise, many can be helped significantly by expectant, thoughtful, spiritually sensitive prayer. Therefore a key part of each session would be the opportunity to pray with someone about the issues raised, especially asking for the Holy Spirit to break the hold of grudges, impatience or rage, and to build new habits of forgiveness, patience and self-control. Such prayer may need to be ongoing over time, making use of people gifted and committed to that task.

As a result, as each week goes by, a sense of real learning takes place, there is mutual encouragement in the growth of virtue, and the delight of discovering changing patterns of behaviour as people find the joy of giving, the liberation of forgiveness, the comfort of patience, or the delights of kindness.

Naturally we do not learn such arts overnight. One session on forgiveness may not heal grudges that have been carefully nursed over many years. It will be important to give this process time, space and prayer. Yet it is important to start somewhere, to start with focused attention on the key characteristics we need to reflect the nature of our Creator. Such formational teaching can only work if it operates within the context of the values we identified earlier: community life, imitation, regular disciplines and openness to the changes suffering can bring. As we saw before, everything in church life needs to be re-evaluated in the light of the crucial task of enabling people to grow into the image of God in Christ. In this context, such a course will find resonances all over church life, in worship, evangelism, regular teaching, practical action in the community and prayer. More importantly, churches and the people who belong to them may find a new God-given sense of purpose, focus and direction.

Our churches and our societies need that desperately. Churches have within them a treasure greater than any other. It is the life of Christ, which can transform our humdrum, self-oriented lives into invigorating likeness to God our Creator. Our societies are crying out for someone or something to offer such a change, to enable us to relate to each other in love, trust and generosity, rather than suspicion, jealousy and envy. We badly need to learn how to exercise our growing power responsibly and wisely. This is perhaps the church's greatest challenge and its highest calling – to become communities capable of making new people, remade in God's image and capable of God-like wisdom, love and goodness, people who are not just physically healthy but spiritually fit and whole.

Notes

1   C. S. Lewis, *Fern Seeds and Elephants, and Other Essays on Christianity* (Glasgow: Collins, 1975), pp. 39–43.

2   The story is found in Matt. 18.23–35.

3   This devastating tale comes in Luke 7.36–50. An excellent commentary that uncovers all the underlying drama of the scene is in Kenneth E. Bailey, *Poet and Peasant and through Peasant Eyes: A Literary-Cultural Approach to the Parables in Luke*, combined edition (Grand Rapids: Eerdmans, 1983), Section II, pp. 1–21.